I0843521

HOW THEY RUINED US

Karen Kellock Ph.D.

Manual for Superior Men

This is a complete theory based on Einstein physics,
Political Psychology, Systems Theory
and Archetypal Psychiatry.

FORMULA

All success attraction
All disease obstruction
All recovery elimination

You must fast on all three

OBSTRUCTIONS:

People
Habit
Food

HOW THEY RUINED US

Public school dumbing is astounding and it's been three generations of this lunacy. They form an echo chamber with cronies then justify violent destruction of enemies. In a social world where creativity's labeled lame, when things go wrong we take the blame. Managing stigma and false accusation takes up half the time of a creative person. The isolate on the narrow path feels guilt and shame but the accepted one, no way. Social Psych: it's the social that created us and we gotta get outa this.

PRINCIPALITIES & POWERS

IT'S PRINCIPALITIES AND POWERS
SINNERS BRING ON THEIR DESTRUCTION
THE HERO AND THE GENIUS
EARLY CANYONS ARE PART OF HEROISM
THE EARLY LIFE OF HEROES IS OBSTACLES
DISCORDANCES PRECEDE GREATNESS
GRATITUDE IS HEALTHY WITH PURITY
HOW MANY TIMES DID YOU DO THE SAME

PRINCIPALITIES & POWERS

IT'S PRINCIPALITIES AND POWERS

Don't anger back to individual resentments but principalities & powers since you were a sinner.

Your lusts attracted creeps: that's the way it works see. Let go of a desire to get back at personalities.

Sin is a magnet to wicked men creeping in. demons. So let go of anger, PTSD & desire for retaliation.

When you sin God's protective hedge is down and the evil world flows in: that's how it works son.

Look back: all resentments stem from a period of sinning. When pure people were nice/grinning.

Accept responsibility for your sinnin' and all will be explained about your season of treason.

SINNERS BRING ON THEIR DESTRUCTION

As a sinner you were a dense idiot and naturally fell into the trap of Satan's minions in that period.

The autonomisms--things you said & did beyond control--brought it on: that's all you need to know.

Wisdom of this interactional process enables you to let go of resentments to your great relief sis.

Your enemies in that period also did things beyond their control: it was a system in your history [old].

I was wracked with resentments until I realized the system when I was a sinner in fragments.

PRINCIPALITIES & POWERS

I brought it all on: it's inevitable when the hedge is down and Satan's helpers are all around.

A silly woman steeped in diverse lusts is bound to draw in creeps to her house: it's almost a must.

THE HERO AND THE GENIUS

The hero often starts in public disgrace. It's cuz he knows no bounds before limits are in place.

The hero's authentic, a mass of primitive desires and instincts before mature and able to think.

He has no sheepish guards on his behavior, he's all in there before he learns to seek God's favor.

With maturity this behavior is just one more thing to be faced & forgotten, to be bagged as mere token.

He does not have the strict inhibitions normal men have for he is genius: a groundbreaker of new paths.

He is dauntless that he is hated as clueless for his faith is in himself not the fickle feelings of masses.

The young hero's main problem is seeking drug solutions to his victimization by other men.

If he can withstand 10,000 being against him without seeking crutches to help him, he's soon won.

EARLY CANYONS ARE PART OF HEROISM

The hero always has an early canyon, a springboard for growth into destiny when all will know him.

Then his school chums and professors who hate this little upstarter who rebels at conventions sir.

PRINCIPALITIES & POWERS

He's too young to know as much as he does and to have a rare viewpoint that parts from what twas.

Without family backing while facing mass detracting he is susceptible to alcohol or drug taking.

To face life without ego-boosting from drugging is a homesick feeling for he has no backing.

THE EARLY LIFE OF HEROES IS OBSTACLES

The early life of a hero is a mass of these obstacles but fortunately for him they build social muscle.

I was that hero & so are you or you wouldn't resonate with these descriptions of being screwed.

If the hero happens to be female the road to greatness is even more rough as I early found out.

Her sisters hate her the most as women are expected to adapt, conform and give in or they're toast.

A champion destined for great things is bound to suffer chastening and a bruising when young see.

A woman to-be great will have to challenge social convention and expectations from men.

DISCORDANCES PRECEDE GREATNESS

These discordances before greatness may take years or decades and then the healing from escapades.

Unless a silver spoon child most heroes don't start their real work until middle aged lest it all fades.

It's like the world is only there to bat down differences but our hero goes thru a meat grinder as it is.

PRINCIPALITIES & POWERS

It teaches them what people are like and builds social muscle to transcend for real discovery, aye.

If a woman has money it's like an energy and the world can smell it. Is she strong enough to keep it?

Is she self-assured enough to not give it to them as they promise everything and flatter her as darlin'?

These obstacles take years to overcome unless fortunate enough to learn it from dad & mom.

I wasn't strong enough to keep my money. Like a dam fool I just wanted to play Big Mommy.

GRATITUDE IS HEALTHY WITH PURITY

You can feel grateful for all God has given you if you keep your nose clean. If not it's a bad scene.

Gratitude is completely health-giving and relaxing. But you gotta be pure to get it: almost sin-free.

Yes, they ruined us and it took years to regain our status but today's another day so just get with it.

Don't waste any more time past-griping. Life is short and you gotta get on with it--you're lucky.

It wasn't this person or that causing your grief but principalities and powers against you see.

If you ever confronted the original culprits who did it they may not even remember the incident.

HOW MANY TIMES DID YOU DO THE SAME

How many times were you out of control, doing destructive things that didn't make sense at all?

PRINCIPALITIES & POWERS

How many times were you grabby, trying to get things out of someone and appearing so shady?

And yet you matured and looking back couldn't believe you were that way: just look to the future.

Understanding how precious life is you dare not waste another minute being angry & pissed.

Just do your great work now and don't look back. That was all training for a great discovery in fact.

The mind takes pictures and stores them away. Now the trick is to only take good pictures ok.

MEMORY OF SCAMMERS

BAGGING OR DELAYING MEMORY
PERCEPTUAL CLEARING FROM BAGGING
BAG FILING SYSTEM
MEMORIES SNEAK UP BUT KEEP UP
LESSON FROM SCAMMERS
AVOID THE ARGUMENTATION
DUMP HIM BEFORE HE DUMPS YOU
BAGGING BRINGS LIGHTNESS
ANGER IS A WASTE OF TIME
THE DISCIPLINE TO STREAMLINE
MOST PEOPLE WILL BE SCAMMERS
NEVER PAY THEM FIRST!
BE EMPTY THEN A TSUNAMI
YOU MUST BE EMPTY BEFORE FULL
A DRASTIC LACK OF CONTINUITY
IT'S NOT THE END BUT THE BEGINNING
NO ONE ELSE COULD HAVE TAKEN IT

MEMORY OF SCAMMERS

BAGGING OR DELAYING MEMORY

Bad memories: I delayed em till noon or put em in a bag to go out later, boom. I recovered, and soon.

When I attacked my bad thoughts--by delaying or bagging--a whole new beautiful world lit up.

No longer being a prisoner of horrible memories opened up a phantasmagoria--I was so happy!

To think I could control sick memories put me in the driver's seat for once, not captured like a dunce.

I put signs up: "DELAY" or "BAG IT" to put memories under my control, not torturing me/making me old.

PERCEPTUAL CLEARING FROM BAGGING

To think I could be happy every minute of the day, not be stung with an embarrassing memory.

Satan would sting me at all times and I wished I was dead: not joy but a suicide thought instead.

PTSD & intrusive thoughts extends original events to the present: it's right here despite many years.

You don't need this, I don't need this and God doesn't want this for us. Follow the plan, be joyous.

If the past was a phase of deep sin, it's a season of treason and memories will be a problem.

MEMORY OF SCAMMERS

All memories from the sin period should be put in their own bag for they ALL will be awful and sad.

Put em all in a bag and after repentance throw the whole bag out. That era don't even think about.

Learn to "catch" the thought before it catches you. Never touch it or it will touch you, whew.

Immediately divert the thought to the bag or the chosen hour to run it thru your mind and be sad.

BAG FILING SYSTEM

Use the "bag" trick as a filing system: this thought goes in the sin era, that one in the divorce era, etc.

The bag-filing system allows you to separate from the emotional impact of the thought problem.

As you follow this corrective routine, remind yourself God wants you to be happy consistently.

There's no way you can be happy re-living the brutal past. It is anti-God: it's the devil in contrast.

The re-lived events made me shudder with anxiety. Thru' the day out of nowhere I was hit see.

Does that sound like God's way? No way, and realizing that makes it easier to follow this plan ok.

Before I knew it I was arguing with the air. Lecturing someone who was dead or gone long before.

MEMORIES SNEAK UP BUT KEEP UP

It sneaks up on you so be assiduous in this new plan. Put signs up and take control of life man.

MEMORY OF SCAMMERS

Stop being angry at the past when you didn't take control or caved into users, one or all.

For that is also the devil's way: to beat you up over the dead past which can never be corrected ok.

Filing the memory to the bag separates you from it. It disconnects the intense emotion doesn't it?

LESSON FROM SCAMMERS

When scammed don't chew the bone with them just block em, pay them off and forget them.

You'll continue getting scammed until you've finally learned your lesson, so thank God for em.

Just pay them off & don't argue anymore. If you stay in that system you'll make mistakes some more.

You lost fifty bucks. Did you trust again & pay em first, smuck? Learn your lesson or have bad luck.

Their karma is coming cuz you won't have a thing more to do with them. Just learn your lesson friend.

To stay in the system telling em how bad they are wastes time: just block and pay em off, aye.

Thank the guy who scammed you last cuz you still had to learn your lesson I guess--now have a blast.

AVOID THE ARGUMENTATION

As long as you stay in the system arguing with them you'll continue making mistakes, time-wastin'.

Pay them off [paying for your lesson] then forget em for their time is coming when you're gone son.

MEMORY OF SCAMMERS

Let em enjoy your money now--when it runs out they'll see you're not around & they messed up, wow.

You'll be so much happier when they're gone it'll be worth losing the money. Block em, you'll see.

They expect you to still try getting your money's worth but you're gone cuz you put SELF first.

Thank God for the last guy who scammed you--if it's the last time you're a sucker it was worth it Sue.

Get rid of the scammers in your life and everything will go smooth and nicely at last [no strife].

DUMP HIM BEFORE HE DUMPS YOU

Dump him before he dumps you or you're back into waiting forever with him in control & clever.

By writing off the fifty he scammed you for and forgetting him, you can now make a million.

When you transcend the scammer rather than arguing forever you feel so much better it's a releaser.

By releasing the scammer rather than hating the rogue bummer everything now comes together.

Look at it this way: you paid to get rid of him [to clear the way of clutter] to now make a million.

You paid fifty lousy bucks to get rid of the chump so it will now change your luck to go WAY up.

Don't waste time being angry at the scammer cuz then he's in control again-- look at that as your sin.

BAGGING BRINGS LIGHTNESS

MEMORY OF SCAMMERS

You feel so much lighter, purer and wiser when rid of the grabby scammer who bugged you forever.

It was worth losing fifty lousy bucks to his grabby hands so you now ascend to the wealthy heavens.

By writing him off despite the loss you dumped the lead that was holding you back, that's a fact.

God forced you to let go of dead weight by letting you be scammed which was the last straw ok.

ANGER IS A WASTE OF TIME

Don't waste time being angry at the scammer cuz then he's in control again and it's like a hammer.

If they come back after paying em off don't take the lure for since they've gone you're too much happier.

Reckless self-destruction often comes with great talent. It's just another era to be overcome.

If one rises like a comet to great fame without the discipline to maintain it ends speedily ok.

If you DARE take the lure again with a scammer thinking he's changed you'll degrade, even derange.

Listen to the kids: all they talk about is the latest material thing--on and on, it's so tedious & boring.

THE DISCIPLINE TO STREAMLINE

They have no discipline to streamline their lives and live humbly with little before achieving the skies.

I don't know where they get their money to buy the latest silly trinkets and to fill their closets.

MEMORY OF SCAMMERS

Before true success and fame one gives away everything. He creates a space, streamlining.

It's called pneumaticity: creating a space for the new to fill in. I'm telling you get rid of everythin'

I gave away everything but just a black camisole. I felt so elegant being free of accumulation y'all.

Scammers are evil. They'll lure you in again then discard you again cuz it's just who they are people.

MOST PEOPLE WILL BE SCAMMERS

Most people are scammers so you gotta cultivate your worker garden: get good at rejecting em.

If you pay em first you'll never see em again or they'll say "they'll do it" in a future fake: reject em man.

You'll pay em first til you learn your lesson so the last scammer was your teacher then that's it man.

You'll lose money to the scammers until you don't anymore. You're paying for your lessons brother.

Thinking the majority are scammers puts em all in a disdained/ignored category you forget forever.

You pay em no mind, they aren't even worth being angry at or being unkind, you just forget em, aye.

NEVER PAY THEM FIRST!

People do stupid things and as soon as you give em the money they forget all they were promising.

Just because they are computer savvy doesn't mean they're not still stuck in blind immaturity.

MEMORY OF SCAMMERS

Blind immaturity: give em the money and they're gone. They're not thinking of anything but wrong.

The reason people seem to becoming less and less is due to your coming success & being blessed.

Not only are you learning about scammers [the biggest category] but you're disciplined & greater.

BE EMPTY THEN A TSUNAMI

It's just like a Tsunami: right before it is the greatest and highest it's the lowest and quietest.

There's no one around, they've all left your side. This is no reason to cry but feel joy, success is nigh.

You're so disciplined there's no one who compares or comes near. It's lonely at the top but don't fear.

Waiting alone is your last test. You planted a great seed: it's hard waiting but you will be blessed.

All of a sudden everyone's either dumb or gone. You're standing as one with nothing but faith alone.

Stop thinking about people cuz they won't do you any good. Just focus on work, understood?

Stress is a major reason for unexplained and sudden weight gain. Being pissed or held down ok.

The immature slough off. They start fired up good enough but then gradually/suddenly they fluff.

Sustained reliability that does not disappoint is a characteristic of the mature man, amen.

YOU MUST BE EMPTY BEFORE FULL

MEMORY OF SCAMMERS

For success you must become EMPTY before getting FULL. You'll have no friends left at all.

It's called pneumaticity: you MAKE A SPACE [by emptying out] then it beautifully fills in see.

You'll go to your email and there's nothing there. That's a sign of mass attractions very soon sir.

It's a weird feeling to be totally empty of friends but not to you cuz you've been schooled, amen.

You're going to a whole new realm transcending all you've known so there's none of the past around.

A DRASTIC LACK OF CONTINUITY

You feel a drastic lack of continuity, the sameness & predictability others crave so much see.

So you fix this by DREAMING of the wonderful future. Your dreams cure present emptiness for sure.

You know you must be empty to attract fullness so you enjoy this creative respite, your hiatus.

Boo hoo, you're so unpopular. No emails or calls but you know what's happening: its the future!

Ha ha ha, you've no emails. Hurray, you know what it means: the future is arriving, your payday.

IT'S NOT THE END BUT THE BEGINNING

It's not the end it's the beginning but feels like nothing. Don't be unhappy, look ahead to great things.

When all leave your side, you feel life is over. This isn't clever since the future is so much bigger.

MEMORY OF SCAMMERS

What distinguishes you so much from others? Events like these, being left with nothing see.

Weaker earthlings gotta have people around all the time but you sir are a champion of God, aye.

You had to be totally cleaned out--every drawer--to be ready for what God's about to do [He pours].

Everything's in reverse. What feels like nothing is the most high thing. Everything is compensating.

NO ONE ELSE COULD HAVE TAKEN IT

No one else could have taken what happened to you. You proved yourself: strong tho' screwed.

The creative act occurs underground before it soon sprouts and brings a giant harvest all around.

You laid a helluva seed but like any farmer you must WAIT for the harvest in complete faith see.

You're too advanced, that's why there's no followers yet but once it HITS everyone will want it friend.

CONTROLLING THOUGHTS

GENIUS IS ISOLATED IN THOUGHTS
PEOPLE CAUSE MENTAL ILLNESS
LINGERING EFFECTS OF YOUR GUESTS
WAKING UP TO WHAT YOU LET IN
DON'T PROJECT PAST ONTO THE PRESENT
CUTTING YOURSELF FREE
YOUR BOAT HAD A HOLE IN IT
MARXIAN TEACHERS & GROUPTHINK
DO-GOODERS OR CAVING TO USERS?
INVASION OF SPIRITUAL UNDERWORLD
INTRUSIVE THOUGHTS [PTSD]
WE DON'T THINK THOUGHTS, WE CHOOSE EM
A WONDERLAND FREE OF PAST THOUGHTS
THE PRESENT IS RUINED BY THE PAST
PUT EM ALL IN A BAG TO GO OUT
THE BAG OF AN ERA OF LAG
GENIUS IS AUSTERE SIMPLICITY

CONTROLLING THOUGHTS

GENIUS IS ISOLATED IN THOUGHTS

Simply put, the more isolated and alone you are the more smart you probably are, a star.

So don't bemoan this temporary feeling of pathetic, hideous isolation, soon you'll have fame son.

Instead of **PTSD** & past resentments, think of all your post-trauma growth since all of that sis.

Thinking back frames you with the past but too much has changed since all that: why go back?

PEOPLE CAUSE MENTAL ILLNESS

The fact is, you **WANTED** them there. You were lonely, a hideous image--you were very immature.

You're not free adapting to other people. Only in solitude does freedom ring: high as a steeple.

They want this, they want that. They ask to borrow money then call you selfish: it's all crap.

Why are you giving up your precious freedom to accommodate your guests? They are pests.

All so you won't be "lonely"? Come on Susie, wake up to reality and let the social go, finally.

For life is but a minute and you have much to accomplish: your guests block all this.

Why be mad at your past invaders? This takes up so much precious time from you, a worker.

CONTROLLING THOUGHTS

LINGERING EFFECTS OF YOUR GUESTS

I wasted years being mad at past invaders. I learned to focus on post-trauma growth instead sir.

Stop lecturing these past introjects too. You're arguing with the air, can't you see they're not there?

Face it: you've no one to blame but yourself. You let em in cuz you were lonely, a stupid/useless elf.

Now don't waste one more minute on these losers from your past. Wake up to the now: have a blast.

Think back to when you were an immature, weak and sycophantic doormat. It's amazing is it not?

Think on this: You're just negative and these feelings "land" on any current event in your present.

WAKING UP TO WHAT YOU LET IN

Take responsibility for your own idiocy for letting in people you couldn't stand. Wake up man.

That was your SPIRIT rearing up but you would listen to it, no you wanted to be a hero to the public.

I recall being a wallflower and ashamed of it. So when they'd come I actually felt complemented.

It didn't matter they were coming to use me for this or that. It never occurred to me about the rats.

It all comes down to these things: you didn't have a life and you weren't self-aware, that's all see.

But now you have a life, now you are busy and productive. So why waste one more minute?

CONTROLLING THOUGHTS

As for those in your life now, if you trust em make a decision to trust em until you can't hon'.

You want a happy life because you deserve it. God wants it for you: to have joy every minute.

Use restraint in buying things too. Everything has an expiration date so learn to purge things Sue.

The people you're mad at were younger then and you were too. It's irrational to recall it and stew.

DON'T PROJECT PAST ONTO THE PRESENT

Don't assume the same things of your current people. Trust em until you can't and relax, that's all.

Ok so you were scammed in the past. You've worked that through & this is a new era with God, alas.

Children of alcoholics are people pleasers so let people in who are users without a thought sir.

A child of an alcoholic lets em walk all over him. They're so used to the abuse it's nothing to them.

Let God be your new Father for He blesses His sons and daughters: you're a king/queen for sure.

It's the daughters of alcoholics who let hobosexuals in to rain on their parade & dewind their sails.

Don't waste time being mad at past invaders. Instead see it's a reflection of alki parents [daughter].

CUTTING YOURSELF FREE

Cut yourself free. Love has to stop somewhere along the line or it's just like committing suicide.

CONTROLLING THOUGHTS

Rather than specific resentments holding you back, realize that most humans are crazy: fact.

You were shocked & stunted at what they did to you but it was you're naiveté that blinded you Sue.

You opened the door to evil, naive about people. You got hurt but that's how you learned it all.

Had you known then what you know now you woulda shut your door but you didn't, that's all.

YOUR BOAT HAD A HOLE IN IT

It's like a boat with a hole in it: the ocean flows in doesn't it? That's evil before you realized it.

I didn't know it either: I trusted em like my brothers & got hurt, scammed & robbed by the clever.

You had to get hurt that way cuz you didn't learn it from mommy and daddy: the human race is scary.

Your liberal mother may have told you to "love everyone" so you just naturally let em in: tragedy.

Christianity is not about loving everybody but drawing lines. We have standards and ethics, aye.

Your liberal mother may have said to "love everyone" so you naturally let em in to your ruin [no fun].

You should forgive evildoers but not forget: you shouldn't let em in again to your detriment.

Because I didn't listen to Dad I got hurt real bad. People just wanna use you so fence up or be sad.

Traumas imprinted from earlier make us cave in later and this is called "mental illness" sir.

CONTROLLING THOUGHTS

MARXIAN TEACHERS & GROUPTHINK

Marxist professors combined with liberal groupthink made us cave in to freaks: what a stink.

Tyranny and treachery made us crazy until we woke up to the difference between us and commies.

It was the communist spirit that flourished, making us give up individuality for the good of social-ist.

Anytime you're asked to give up your wants for the good of the whole, that's the commie spirit y'all.

They are so conceited and arrogant in what they want from us: learn to stand up against scuzz!

It's bad enough they use you for a restaurant, now they ask to borrow money too? Shut them out.

DO-GOODERS OR CAVING TO USERS?

So you're a do-gooder. Learn to distinguish between honest charity and caving in to users.

Do you want applause/acclaim from man [fleeting fame then nothin'] or love of God, the Head One?

People will do anything for approval, making fools of themselves then God wants their removal.

I caved into users thinking I was doing good until they took me for everything, then I understood.

The user will rob the one who's helping him not the ones who are wise, they won't ever let him in.

The swindler scams the one who's helping him not the others, they're too smart to call him brother.

CONTROLLING THOUGHTS

It's the wallflower who needs approval who lets in the smiling robber who flatters then takes you.

It's your home--your space & sanctuary--so why let in those who just wanna hang and use thee?

INVASION OF SPIRITUAL UNDERWORLD

There's a spiritual underworld that's dark & dirty. Detach from drip-dry hangers, set yourself free.

First they come without calling, then they use you then they start to give advice: it's insulting.

You may fear loneliness if you get rid of users and phoniness but I promise you'll be blessed.

The most important advice a mother could give a daughter is BOUNDARIES and none other.

Any man who asks a woman for money is a gigolo and should be shown the door: JUST GO!

There's nothing more disgusting than a weak female lending a man money to get his approval.

He's weak, she's weak and they deserve each other. What a sick system as they go down together.

There's nothing more attractive than she who stands up for herself. Not angrily just the velvet glove.

INTRUSIVE THOUGHTS [PTSD]

The most important thing about managing intrusive thoughts is to delay them to a time slot.

The PTSD thoughts are noxious so we DELAY them to a certain time each day to feel that anxious.

CONTROLLING THOUGHTS

Instead of hammered with thoughts as they come up, delay them to a certain time to be beaten up.

Intrusive thoughts cause anxiety & racing heart. It's the devil's way of wrecking the day from the start.

I was beaten up each day/all day by thoughts of half a life ago. How silly to be a victim/let this go.

Just when I was happy a negative thought would pop up. This is the devil so delay it and look up.

WE DON'T THINK THOUGHTS, WE CHOOSE EM

We don't THINK thoughts, we CHOOSE them as they stream by: wanting to be mad at somebody.

You get so used to being mad at something happening at 20 it makes a groove that we repeat see.

Giving into intrusive thoughts becomes a vicious, deadening habit. Decide to be done with it.

With intrusive thoughts Satan used me as a punching bag that would whip me/hold me back.

Establish new habits: instead of feeling thoughts, practice DELAYING them to a time slot.

Always remember it's Satan doing it. A loving God would never consign you to sadly feeling it.

You'll feel so much better controlling thoughts. You were their slave before as life turned to rot.

A WONDERLAND FREE OF PAST THOUGHTS

Try to enjoy each minute and as intrusive thoughts come up consign them to the outer limits.

CONTROLLING THOUGHTS

Why be ruled by a bitter past? The past is gone, the Tao moves on and the present is pure joy at last.

Here I was sitting in luxury and away from the treachery but it was as if I was still back there see.

Don't waste your latter years chewing on the former years. The losers are gone, enjoy new peers.

THE PRESENT IS RUINED BY THE PAST

Here I was in a starry, never-better present but plagued by a scary, never-worse past, totally spent.

God doesn't want this for us: being constantly pestered by thoughts of a dead past filled with fuss.

Choose a time then practice saying to yourself: "I'll feel this at noon". Practice: delay it then swoon.

Without those thoughts your life would be a wonderland. Just think of that: mentally expand.

Here I was, sitting in retirement in a luxury mansion but held down by thoughts of losers and scum.

It's our **THOUGHTS** that create our reality more than our actualy surroundings of luxury vs. poverty.

What a life-changing revelation this truly is if we can finally get it: delay em til later or forget it.

What a wonderful fantasy land your life would be without intrusive thoughts of the past see.

When thoughts arise image a big sign that says "DELAY!" and you'll be ok for another fascinating day.

PUT EM ALL IN A BAG TO GO OUT

CONTROLLING THOUGHTS

Another trick to ridding thoughts is putting em all in a bag then throwing the whole bag out.

Instead of individual resentments of this guy or that, put it in your bag that's going out full of brats.

Concentrate on every moment being happy: either by throwing the bag out or delaying thoughts.

Since thoughts sneak up we gotta learn to focus: on delaying or bagging then it's all ok with us.

THE BAG OF AN ERA OF LAG

We put the thoughts in a bag cuz it was an era of lag: the whole phase was bad due to our lack.

It's a dark blackout: the people we knew and the events that accrued--an era of mistakes and feuds.

Put em ALL in the bag. Don't waste time resenting each one, the whole phase was a terrible drag.

We get so used to getting mad [stuck in the memory groove of all bad] we find things that are sad.

Don't waste precious latter years with this crap of always going back. Learn these tricks or stay sad.

We all have canyons before success: why should we focus on that mess rather than being blessed?

If the plan doesn't work, change the plan. But this one WILL work if you do it daily/religiously man.

Every time you cringe with a bad thought you deepen the groove compelling you to repeat it all.

GENIUS IS AUSTERE SIMPLICITY

CONTROLLING THOUGHTS

Small minds tend to add while big minds tend to subtract: they're always simplifying: fact.

De-cluttering is essential, always, while adding to the superfluity is characteristic of the normies.

The high class have a few things of high quality while the rabble have many of the cheap see.

Learn to ruthlessly purge non-essentials. Lead a simple life eliminating what you don't need: simplify.

Eliminating what you don't need allows focusing on what you do and this amplifies the whole stew.

Genius is austere simplicity, contrary instincts, deviant associations and clearsighted audacity.

One meal a day: Why go back into digestion when all that energy could stay in the head, THINKIN'?

HOW THEY RUINED US

GO BEYOND PEOPLE
CREATIVITY AND OPEN WOUNDS
MOTHER WOUNDS
PUBLIC PUT DOWNS
RELATIONAL CHOICES FROM HEAD
FORGETTING WHO YOU ARE
JOY OF RELEASING SOUL TIES
RELIEF TRANSCENDING A PROBLEM
EMOTION AND THE LION'S DEN
SEE BEYOND MERE ATTRACTION
PSYCHOPATHIC NARCISSISTS
VICTIMS FEEL GUILTY
FLY ABOVE LIKE A BIRD
PUSH SELF BLAME OUT
MONKEY BARS
A POISON WAS POURED IN
SPIRIT OF EXHAUSTION
ENTITLED AND LACKING EMPATHY
THEY FORGOT WHAT YOU TOLD THEM
SOCIAL MAKES EM MENTALLY ILL
BEHAVIOR CUED IN SOCIAL CONTEXT
FILTHY CULTURAL CRAMDOWNS
THE LOVING FALSE CHURCH
WE KILLED A SAINT/REJECTED A GENIUS
SOCIALISTS NEVER SLEEP
POPULATION REPLACEMENT FOR POWER
BEYOND THE PALE
A TIME OF MENTAL/SPIRITUAL DRAUGHT
WOMEN WILL RUIN A SISTER
THINK: MAGIC CARPET RIDE
UNCONTROLLABLY MOODY MOTHERS
FEMININE FLAW
INNER CRITIC
LOSS OF AUDACITY
SELF-LOVE IS: BOUNDARIES
FEMINIST SEXUALIZATION OF KIDS
SHAMELESS DEBAUCHERY
TYRANNY OF THE GROUP

HOW THEY RUINED US

SMARTER MEANS LESS POPULAR
PURITANISM: A RESPONSE TO CHAOS
FAMOUS KNOW-NOTHINGS
THEY'RE ALL DUMBED DOWN
COPYING MEN IS NOT FEMALE POWER
PSYCHOLOGY OF GANGS
HAUGHTINESS SHALL BE BROUGHT LOW
GOD KILS GIANTS WHO ARE AFTER US
TYRANTS FEAR THE BIBLE
WHEN WICKED RULE THE PEOPLE MOURN
LIBERAL IDEOLOGY TRUMPS LOGIC
A COUNTRY GOING INTO JUDGMENT
FEMINIST ADVICE RUINS LIVES
LIBERALS ARE LAWLESS
TYRANNY OF THOUGHT
TOLERANT GENERATIONS THE MOST INTOLERANT
BEING POSITIVE IS SELECTIVE DIS-ATTENTION
PHARMACUCIA IN AMERICA
INSANITY IS A LOWER ARCHETYPE
TO LIBERALS ENDS JUSTIFY MEANS
SCANDALS ASIDE THEY STILL LOVE POWERS THAT BE
BE SCARED OF DENSE
THEY JUST KNOW THEY'RE RIGHT
FROM THE SIXTIES: SLOPPY, DIRTY, UNPRETTY
SATANISTS WANT TO CONTROL EVERYONE
POLITICANS GROVEL TO HOLLYWOOD SCUM
THEY SAY "PEACE" THEN DESTRUCTION COMES SWIFTLY
LEFTISTS ARE NOT "HUMANITARIANS"
TRENDIES LOVE DECADENCE
SIGNS OF TYRANNY CREEP
HIGH-CAR/B/LOW-FAT AND FIT?
HIGH ON REVERSAL DIETING
GLYCATION: MEATS ARE AGING
HIGH ON NO-FAT
MEATS ARE AGING
RICE, CORN AND BARLEY
SUGAR IS THE FUEL
TERSE VERSE BEFORE INTERFERENCE

HOW THEY RUINED US

GO BEYOND PEOPLE

Things go wrong, we take the blame. That's the result of living in a social world where creativity's labeled lame.

Managing uncomfortable stigma and false accusation takes up half the time of a creative person.

Anyone different is likely to be stigmatized. STIGMA is near impossible to live down, despised.

The isolated genius on the narrow path feels the guilt and shame but the accepted one, no way.

I call it SOCIAL PSYCH. It's to remind us it's the SOCIAL that created us and we gotta get outa this.

The culture is getting coarse and every day it's worse. Focus on purity and simplicity as your major purpose.

They can be so beautiful and powerful then like a wilted flower be gone forever cuz it's all about sin sir.

Allow yourself to go beyond this little man giving you no attention. It's the next fella you'll be lovin'.

What to do when the mother says "I just hate you"--clamp self-expression and hide in cocoon.

Good and evil has a wide gulf between them but schools teach it's all the same, like every man's your friend.

CREATIVITY AND OPEN WOUNDS

Description of my history: they had all the power and now they don't so I'm happily free.

HOW THEY RUINED US

The ravenous beast inside was the devil clear and simple. He's outa you now so forget it girl.

The greatest saints WERE the worse sinners. Consider that for a moment: this insight's a winner.

Slobbering lovers and virtue signallers won't be there when you need em--just notice this.

The worse you were the greater you are now: they can't see both sides of a gestalt so no worries gal.

To be creative you must be OPEN but that means you're an OPEN WOUND to lil' demons rushing in.

Tell people: one is traumatized by how cruel ones are to YOU for what your mother did TO YOU.

"But it's your mother" they scream when broaching topic of the mother wound--you shut up faster.

All mothers are kind, loving and gentle--this mom-saint image is farthest from the truth ya know.

It's a worldwide fairy tale about nice mothers and ignored topic of when they're unfit for sure.

I know the trauma and aftermath of spending a life in a system of abuse, expecting to be used.

Bullying and shaming is a choice so let's not make an excuse for this narcissistic mother too.

MOTHER WOUNDS

The mother wound is the deep pain from being gaslit, ostracized, bullied, shamed and blamed.

The painful spirit of confusion is the outcome, a system of secret coalitions and put-downs in sum.

HOW THEY RUINED US

Parentification: You're forced to mother your mother. She's dependent but then sides with others.

Just to defend yourself you're forced to grow up fast but having lost your childhood you lack depth.

She was supposed to parent. But did she really parent or did she just abuse you? Feel, think, stew.

Then the siblings--flying monkeys--chime in with the same rude gossipings--she's blocked/unfree.

It's not lack of mothering but never having a real mother just an enemy destroying your rep see.

PUBLIC PUT DOWNS

A narc mother puts down her daughter standing next to her right in front of others, a psych killer.

The narc mother will fabricate facts to justify her malicious toxic words, actions and behavior.

Narcissism make people cruel, cunning and spiteful--just cross them once and you'll get an earful.

They are highly critical especially of spouses and children and the marks remain in them.

A narcissist feels superior to others and has no empathy, using manipulations of treachery.

To heal mother wounds we must first get the facts about what a narcissist is and how they wreck us.

It's heartbreaking how many relate to the movie Mommie Dearest, a mother who's a narcissist.

Knowing God is real on a personal level is the shift we need to change this relational scenario.

HOW THEY RUINED US

RELATIONAL CHOICES FROM HEAD

Make relational choices from head and note how your esteem leak attracts the walking dead.

Where was that leak in self esteem allowing an inferior into your heart? Think now and mark it.

God washes away an avalanche of thoughts saying you're inferior--now see his toxic actions dear.

Give the world the best version of you and the world always gives back matching energy too.

You teach the world how to treat you by the way you treat yourself and it's like heaven vs. hell.

You **NEED** those responses so put yourself together as you did at your highest points whenever.

FORGETTING WHO YOU ARE

You forgot who you were. Now put your energy out there to get responses to you, the preferred.

After getting away from a fool like that saying no one will want you, it's good to hear your value.

When you put yourself together others articulate your value but can tell when you're slipping too.

Get outa the sweatpants signalling your depression and get some makeup on: transcend that con.

This proves the value of going no-contact, since the mere interaction is enough to wreck it.

Even dealing with tech guys from foreign countries and work habits brought this feeling of lunacy.

JOY OF RELEASING SOUL TIES

HOW THEY RUINED US

After releasing a powerful soul tie like that you feel so good as the joy of the Lord is your strength.

Just ask and the power of God lifts your spirit from the anguish and confusion--the demons fear it.

You need your spirit revived in this situation. You feel hit by a tidal wave but suddenly it lifts hon.

Even brief interactions with tech guys can bring this overwhelming feeling, it's a spirit honey

You need to say "Lord I'm on the edge, this has done something to me I can't explain" and He'll oblige.

RELIEF TRANSCENDING A PROBLEM

The relief of going beyond a problem, transcending cobweb illusions and low self-esteem resulting.

Recall the feelings of confusion/exhaustion. Then when relieved the utter joy of mental expansion.

A toxic relationship drains you spiritually so being separate while God works on it is healing.

Stop making relational choices based on the body too--destroying your life by the chemistry of fools.

Consider your ways. You keep coming up empty carrying a bag with holes and so unhappy.

Go back in history to analyze "type". Did they not ALL drain you and wreck your self esteem, aye?

If I make relational choices based on emotion I'm a great candidate for full-time control/manipulation.

EMOTION AND THE LION'S DEN

HOW THEY RUINED US

Did you leap into the lion's den on pure emotion when your brain was yelling to turn back around?

Where were you more emotional than cerebral, feeling a romantic magnetic pull before your fall?

Analyze your mind--where was the leak to self-esteem allowing you to open your heart to a fiend?

Analyze your psyche--what was it that allowed an inferior into your heart to then break it?

You must go on relationship lockdown and let God heal your spirit before going to another man.

You must deny that romantic magnetic pull with all your might. Pray for God to release the soul tie.

SEE BEYOND MERE ATTRACTION

See beyond mere attraction. Don't get stuck there and see beyond the little man to his great plans.

BEWARE of all romantic pulls. The magnetism is crazy and he's all you think about now: no go.

The worse you were before the more astounding your greatness now--let detractors eat crow!

Consciousness squeezes out a pearl and then I write it down and if I can't I'm greatly concerned.

Key to writing is waiting: WAIT for the pearl to rise to the surface/bubble up-- THEN you write it

What does it take to get away? Knowledge: getting hep vs. being hooked. Like a naive girl: yuk.

He was always secretly planning what he'd do to me next to make me batty as hell and desperate.

HOW THEY RUINED US

He's always planning new secret devices to make her desperate as sadism always increases.

PSYCHOPATHIC NARCISSISTS

With the psychopathic narcissist you're always waiting for the other shoe to drop/cruelty nonstop.

Of course anyone that close with an intention of controlling gets into her deepest psyche.

He has a familiar spirit seeming so uncanny the way he "knows" everything: the knot is tightening.

He puts ideas in her mind and then it happens. He reads her mind too, seeming so amazin'

It's a demonic relationship. The culprit abuses her for something to happen in the near future.

VICTIMS FEEL GUILTY

The victim of the narcissist even wakes up feeling guilty and ashamed, just for being human ok.

The insecure infants are terrified of so much freedom in what we're sayin' like its a catastrophe brewin.

Conservative voices are breaking out of the leftist media bubble--the batty commie echo chamber.

If you oppose illegal immigration the liberals call you a "white nationalist" if you can believe this.

TO BE INSPIRED: never force the fit but wait for the creative impulse which comes through us.

It overwhelms a consciousness with no tools to deal with it--the energy leaks into sex/theft.

HOW THEY RUINED US

An event that is so noxious, toxic, overwhelming and debilitating we call it severe trauma see.

FLY ABOVE LIKE A BIRD

Instead of constantly feeling to blame, guilty and ashamed just see how far above you came.

It definitely helps seeing how far you transcend the multitudes stuck in a social hypnotic stew.

Writing 18 hours a day because it's a life calling from God after trauma and being seen as odd.

Guilt and shame for going to the bathroom, for having thoughts of lust or any human inclination.

The second result from toxic relationship is the guilt and shame for being human--can you imagine?

It starts in the family--inherited guilt and shame--then gains its own momentum as time goes on.

PUSH SELF BLAME OUT

The feeling of self blame must be pushed outa your soul and spirit, it's an inputed form of lunatic.

When talking to yourself, own your part. Repent then say "this is the way it is" and then restart.

Here's where you must talk to yourself: "This is not my fault, my sense of unworthiness is imposed."

These toxic thoughts work against the best version of us, the healthy daughter/son of God.

Paul says to cast down imaginations/pull down strongholds: cut these thoughts off now.

HOW THEY RUINED US

When those moods hit saying you're the worst person in the world you think he's all you deserve.

MONKEY BARS

They use monkey bars: they swing out to make you desperate then swing back in to re-addict.

A narcissist has no empathy: he can't see what he's doing to thee he's all for his self see.

You've been repeating the scene. Abandoned and then reclaimed then bashed again and again.

Toxicity all day long and you never know. He's with you then ghosts you then pops up from below.

The narcissist gaslit you intentionally making you feel you're losing it and now you're feeling it.

Your feelings are a boiling caldron trying to find a logical explanation for an illogical situation.

Dealing with a narcissist has been an impossible situation since he can't see beyond self.

A POISON WAS POURED IN

A terrible poison was poured into your spirit on a regular basis and you didn't know you were sick.

After the breakup all the stuff submerged with denial comes out and she blames herself.

Maybe you've had multiple toxic relationships so listen to this: stop blaming yourself sis.

But Samson's hair began to grow again. You will come out of hypnotism/not be stuck in depression.

HOW THEY RUINED US

A toxic relationship robbed Samson of his identity, purpose, sight and strength [gift from God].

It wrecks the rest of their days and pollutes every relationship moving forward completely.

SPIRIT OF EXHAUSTION

One's been disempowered like the life has been sucked right out and many never recover at all.

Exiting the toxic relationship leaves one exhausted and disconnected--how to come back centered?

You don't have a spring in your step as before, you're not optimistic and alert, your spirit's poor.

You've been broken, weakened and compromised emotionally and it's affected your personality.

A female narcissist will equally exhibit these core characteristics and cause as much damage.

ENTITLED AND LACKING EMPATHY

Entitled, lacking empathy and exploitative while feeling superior--of all narc traits those are core.

Its your job to fit inside their mold so they stress the notion of "agreement" and "adaptability".

Signs of a trauma bond: a high control relationship with strong opinions but never any adjustments.

For years people may say "you've no need to apologize" because you're still in a mental trap, aye.

Things like defending yourself or explaining way beyond necessity may last awhile after that guy.

HOW THEY RUINED US

You choose to live a life of introspection and the narcissist does not--so what, move on

They blameshift, tell lies and keep secrets keeping a very thick wall between them and us all.

They always use denial: I didn't do that, you got that wrong, hell if it was my fault--you know the spiel.

Narcissists won't accept input at basic levels. Another interpretation's enough to arouse the devil.

"I just need you to go along with me cuz I'm the smart one in the room and don't forget it."

Narcissists commit to false superiority: a great deal of entitlement sprinkled with one-up comments.

They don't wanna take the time to know you, that's how they operate. It's more get outa my way ok.

There's no blending with anyone different from them it's get outa here with no attempt to understand.

THEY FORGOT WHAT YOU TOLD THEM

They forgot what you told them yesterday, they're just not sensitive to you save you aggravate.

They make no attempt to know or understand you from the inside out--it's them not anyone else.

The callous have very low levels of empathy--a blank stare or questioning how you think see.

Their anger is so dysregulated you never know when it'll pop up in secret and destructive antics.

The anger is aggravatingly passive-aggressive: I won't do what you want, only on my terms: sick.

HOW THEY RUINED US

The concept of self-love [no matter what] is a curse as it skips over repentance: building self-worth first.

I don't wanna get into specifics about a person but fly above like a bird. Transcend details/stay clear.

SOCIAL MAKES EM MENTALLY ILL

It's because they're so social that they're mentally ill--it's an echo chamber that gets more filled.

Self-indulgent children see opposing views as villains. "Privilege" is a way of shutting us up: this is racism.

Entitlement society has created the war: The more you claim victimhood the better off you are.

Insofar as Millennials believe in open borders they're the most insane and suicidal generation ever.

Where immorality rules all romance is gone out of life. This isn't charming it's just sensual, rife.

They'll block all views that challenge their own! Remember that to stay on top (on your throne).

There's no lukewarm. If someone's not your friend they're your enemy as we're losing civility.

As things get more urgent the news gets more bland. It maintains mass denial, man.

As our freedoms lessen we learn the lesson of true genius through time: God has risen so keep on pressin'.

You're supposed to learn from mistakes in the first phase not labor over them the rest of your days.

Are they overly friendly? Trying to win your confidence too quickly or WAY too personal sonny?

HOW THEY RUINED US

You experienced Jezebel, the bat outa hell, the dingbat spell and one depedestalled now forget it all.

Ok you experienced the insincere dangerous Jezebel--now you've had that lesson forget it all.

No matter what you say he buds in. Override, override, override. This cannot stand, it's impolite.

BEHAVIOR CUED IN SOCIAL CONTEXT

Polite when alone, he'd fall into his bag when with others by talking over me or whatever.

He wants the limelight on him. No matter what you say he'll interrupt/bud in to redirect attention.

Behavior is cued-in-context. When in a social matrix out comes a different guy in our midst.

When bad behavior is cued in social context the spouse seeks to isolate them to preserve happiness.

FILTHY CULTURAL CRAMDOWNS

Having had ideology cram-downed the youth are just stupid. No light in their eyes, insipid.

It's one thing to not offend but another to approve. You're to hate what God hates/remove.

The false church approves of behavior acceptable to sick society. That's how you tell honey.

The false church won't condemn those bad things God hates if society thinks it's all-ok.

Having been made to accept bad things one loses reason & logic and the results are tragic.

HOW THEY RUINED US

IQ is lowered by accepting lies as truth. Like wanting open borders or abortion up to birth.

THE LOVING FALSE CHURCH

I'm sick of the "loving" false church approving of disgusting things for approval of earthlings.

The new church won't mention sin so as not to offend nor hell where they're all going still.

I'm for returning to holy roller hellfire preaching on sin and repentance, hell and heaven!

Stay with the one you're with & when looking for help it's in your midst. Dad said these would selfix.

The mean narcissist has low self-awareness: that means low empathy and high arrogance.

They are gross in their disrespect and they're not at all bashful about letting you know that.

The narcissist isn't aware enough to know he thinks "someone's gotta pay" for his own pain.

Narcissists are all about compensation for hurt/how they view the world, not nurturing you girl.

"I have to be in control so no one can control me": that is what narcissism is all about see.

Since everything is about winning or losing to the narcissist you're the recipient of his nastiness.

Stay distant with aristocratic reserve. Don't go into who you are but keep afar and thank your stars.

Unchanging gameplan: Stay mute while planning exit strategy and make connections now honey.

HOW THEY RUINED US

Iron sharpens iron but in my case a buncha young thugs did it as I became my best in reaction.

As a boy it makes you happy to have the confidence of an older person but reject molestation son.

Get too close to the truth and they ban you. Don't take it on, it happens to saints & geniuses too.

WE KILLED A SAINT/REJECTED A GENIUS

"Lord help us we killed a saint". That's always how it is so recall this when they accuse and point.

They scorned, mocked and belittled me all my life. Now I'm safe I write about it day and night.

Kings of the earth collude together to bring down God's superior people from their protectors.

You gotta hang in there, they basically hate your guts but don't know why--it's Who's inside of us.

Oh, not supposed to say "superior" as if God and devil are equals, the mythology of liberals.

Socialists promise everything by taking your money but you get only what they wanna give you see.

People in the fifties weren't so instantly chummy. After a world war they knew man has enemies.

They'd been thru a world war where millions were killed so the fifties were restrained not fullabull.

Illegals paid half a million for breaking the law. You can't make this stuff up/they'll never be gone.

I like maturity but you act like a child [cracked] or someone needing their faced slapped.

HOW THEY RUINED US

SOCIALISTS NEVER SLEEP

When word goes out they got half a million for border breaking the whole world will be coming.

Just as long as we don't talk politics we're not banned but we can discuss crazy humans man.

What's happening in California: Big stores shut down rather than being legally robbed <$950.

If you're not in lock-step with the far left on whatever their agenda is today you're fair game.

We gotta stop illegal immigration so American jobs go to American workers: what a no-brainer!

We patriots are not anti-vax but anti-unconstitutional mandate despite being fired or hated.

I know what you've been through being lied on, gossiped about/slandered, I've been there.

Jesus made you white as snow. Your only problem is thinking you're still sullied from below.

POPULATION REPLACEMENT FOR POWER

Whites seek absolution for sins they didn't commit, blacks sympathy for crimes they didn't endure.

Someone seeking a better life is not an "asylum seeker" which was strictly defined previously.

90% of the world is seeking a better life but ASYLUM means escaping persecution and strife.

It's pure Marxism: Demonize the rich then politicians come in to rob Peter to pay Paul to fix em.

HOW THEY RUINED US

It's unthinkable paying a burglar for the "psychological trauma" during the crime. Tom Cotton

Socialists are inherently greedy. They aren't about the people but control, for example see A.O.C.

Socialism is about taking other people's money. It's called greed so liberals are bad company.

If you came here legally you don't get a penny but if you crashed our gates it's half a million honey.

They're irresponsible & childlike: Yah we want all these things but why not more? Let's triple it!

Hopefully they'll push it so much to their downfall, if we aren't captured before as America falls.

Liberal females say "its wonderful, all this spending as America's remade in a new beginning."

BEYOND THE PALE

Things go so far beyond the pale you can't even get mad. Don't argue or be sad just release the cads.

Dear Father: Open the eyes of the people to see this evil to return to freedom, high as a steeple.

Why are bullies a problem? Why are people getting mean? It's due to family breakdown making fiends.

If they're like this now (crude, rude) what'll it be like when there's no food? I'm just sayin': You must seclude.

Everything's about to change. The shocks may amaze so hold on to what's real and avoid the deranged.

False religion is used by authority acting like the devil. That's communitarianism: all is leveled.

HOW THEY RUINED US

They are despicable white witches always virtue signaling for approval--that's ALL they do and it's dangerous.

To create I must have that click in my head. I don't have that click if there is mendacity in the environment.

A TIME OF MENTAL/SPIRITUAL DRAUGHT

In a time like this of spiritual/mental drought there's another modern syndrome: they don't care a lot.

I shuddered living in a liberal town of mental drought--they were shallow and I mal-adapted to no-depth.

They didn't care about a thing and any involvement suddenly messed up life, filled with confusion/strife.

The women were so jealous of each other, instantly flaring up and developing an army against any new one.

As toxic as this environment was any drinking as a device to avoid anxiety instantly brought ruin--stay sober.

The women were absolutely brutal, mean and gossiping. It's called murdering one's reputation: CALUMNY.

Even her friends would needle her or lead her wrong. She's a traitor if it suits her though she appears to belong.

WOMEN WILL RUIN A SISTER

A woman will ruin her own sister if jealousy is the basis of her being bitter. Greek dramas re: the family litter.

The men were awful but the women were far more awful. Mean and spiteful, not good female models.

These people love to get violent so proceed with caution while laying your boundary: walk away gently.

HOW THEY RUINED US

The female genius ends up alone. She can't trust men but she can't trust women more: that's her throne.

A female genius has so had it she won't take a chance on rejection and thus she does not act before him.

By the time the female genius finally reaches success she is war exhausted having fought these resistances.

RACISM is alive and well in America but it's not whites against blacks but blacks against white people.

RACISM is alive and well in America but it's not against blacks but blacks and whites against white people.

White liberals hating white people: putting down their own is traitorship. Look it up: traitors are low shit.

Refuse to be stashed, a definite sign of disrespect. Don't ever be compartmentalized--kept separate.

Never make someone a priority if they only make you an option. Don't be a side dish: that's stashin'

They should be proud of you and if they're not, why are they with you? I'd ask that, fix the problem or be blue.

We're a servant to our dreams not society's expectations but to uphold them they get angry and I run.

THINK: MAGIC CARPET RIDE

Think: magic carpet ride, like you just won the lotto, like you're going to heaven and can't recall anyone at all.

When I leave this world so too all MEMORY is gone. Think of that: the things bugging you now all pass on.

Just enjoy each day and don't take things too seriously cuz in a couple weeks they won't even exist, truly.

HOW THEY RUINED US

DEM CON: The star of the evening was professional teleprompter reader Barrack Hussein Obama.

In my slight slip into people worship I realized how easily I give away my power to them without knowing it.

All that anger was from mother but always remember she got it from her mother, maybe an alcoholic father.

For years it seems, nothing's happening. Then there comes a **POINT** in time where it all changes **SUDDENLY.**

The outcast is also the savant elf on the side. As you're squeezed out don't take rejection as a sign.

Default norm: Burn rainbow flag, get arrested for hate crime. Burn an American flag: no big thing, get nothing.

The hypocritical virtue signaling called political correctness is dying steadily. Most are sick of this/will vote our guy.

Think of it: You prove yourself and now you have to do it again. President Donald Trump

Childhood trauma is any adverse experience altering how he functions in the world: insane boys and girls.

The early trauma can be something the child witnessed or can even occur while in the womb at first.

Many mothers are angry while pregnant. Hormonal shifts affect mental health and she gets indignant.

UNCONTROLLABLY MOODY MOTHERS

An uncontrollably moody and irritable mother has an effect on a sensitive child as even the gentlest goes wild.

A moody mother swings from maudlin to demanding respect and boastin' to angry brawlin' in a moment: momma!

HOW THEY RUINED US

"If momma ain't happy ain't no one's happy" as a contentious female drip-drips until everyone's a dam lunatic.

Mom hated my studying or attending to anything but her. She interrupted me constantly blocking my star.

The child is traumatized both in physical brain changes and spiritual blockages. I was a walking robot sis.

The trauma occurs before the child has the tools to handle or understand it. The personality fragments: a nut.

The parent isn't training the child to be more likable, only more trouble--so he feels hated by the world too.

TRAUMA alters the structure of the brain and the hormones in the body. Culture clash does this suddenly.

You insidious witch. You've caused me more trouble than I've ever known--don't come near my home.

FEMININE FLAW

I can spend a ton of money or I can live on nothing--content cuz it's all the same to me, either way I'm happy.

Feminine Flaw is: advocating for things that destroy their relationship. Think of that, it explains a bagashit.

Sorry, I'm a chronic grouch. I complain too much/set boundaries--for that they hate me/want me out.

He loves her cuz she's young, it's nothing she's done. That's the age: not about merit but the group you're in.

According to them you complain too much and are never happy--you should be grateful for them, the nutty.

Due to relational dysynchrony women will be getting cats. I can sure see that, they're adorable as it gets.

HOW THEY RUINED US

3 pumpernickel with grape spread, shredded wheat with rice milk, raisins/banana/collagen/sucrose, FAST.

Why pumpernickel? It's the ONLY bread that binds acid or mucus, not create it. But is it really it?

Greatest realization: No one cares and you're gonna die no matter. Now just live each day and no more.

Trying to come up with something clever to say and suffering cuz you didn't-- that's the social world isn't it.

A man should choose a woman who's a good homemaker already then he can just move on into it.

INNER CRITIC

The inner critic starts with mom and it kicks our butt up and down as it's incessant, judgmental, unruly.

The inner critic will run all over you causing psych pain, self-sabotage, wrong decisions, missed opportunities.

You shoulda done this or that: that's the inner critic we wish to stop in its tracks. NOTICE when it overtakes.

When this happens you must learn to talk to yourself with compassion, honor, respect and caring.

Keep saying: Give yourself a break today. Always react to that scathing critic with compassion and leeway.

My inner critic starts in with bad memories of the dead and embarrassing past so I practice standing against.

Another way to combat the inner critic is to say "I am perfectly imperfect and basically I'm ok."

Embarrassing memories: It wasn't me, it was when the devil was in control. Anything can happen then, see?

HOW THEY RUINED US

Learn to stand up to the inner bully in your brain cuz that's what the inner critic is. Tell him/her to GTH.

When she drank it's an immediate sensation of being taken over. Relieving at first, then bedlam/disorder.

Putting on my make-up the voice would say "who do you think you are" and i'd say "stop--I'm a star".

You shoulda done this or that--that's called Shoulding on Self and it's always a template from the past to let go.

How can we get anywhere if we're constantly ripping ourself to shreds with inner bully tactics? Kick em out.

God can disempower you in a minute. It's a sudden deflation and I'd hate to witness it or repeat it.

A person facing death wants to maximize every moment. We should all work hard/have that temperament.

LOSS OF AUDACITY

I lost my audacity years ago, realizing they could hit me gave me the right comportment like as if I know.

Now you take that magic carpet ride you always envisioned but only now are eligible for having repented.

To end remorse, realize your sin was a **COPING DEVICE** in that dense/evil environment and leave it at that.

No one cares what you did they're too into their own gig but memory is warped thru shame of an outcast.

The recovered bulimic said "it was more like something happening TO me, an outside force instead."

You think what no one has ever thought before. That makes you rare so keep thinking/putting it out there.

HOW THEY RUINED US

Being in a constant state of anxiety I could not identify his bullying tactics to lay down and be weak.

It's a human drive to distinguish our selves in some way but in some it's an urgent matter of survival.

To make his own way lest he be swept up into the family consciousness of total and strict conformity.

Why people settle: because they're lazy, think it's their best option or they're fearful.

Their fear of being alone is greater than their fear of agony and pain in a bad rel/gruesome twosome.

I never read newspapers cuz they were boring--there's a common Russian feeling: "if it's big it's a lie."

How to create the future: Every time a bad memory pops up replace it instead with a future desire.

Then you create a new future rather than repeat the past over and over. Remember: replace these memories.

SELF-LOVE IS: BOUNDARIES

What exactly is self-love? To me it's BOUNDARIES: laying them and asserting them so the self can thrive.

I suffered the social tyranny of you living next to me and I shudder at the thought of your stupid cruelties.

He'll be able to see thru signs and symbols whether you're right or not. Rely on that, it's from God.

FEMINIST SEXUALIZATION OF KIDS

Schools sexualize our kids! It starts as early as four as they're taught to do nasty things by the libs.

HOW THEY RUINED US

Though against an immoral movement doesn't mean you hate women just those spouting vermin.

He's a foul-mouthed lecherous fool--does that give him power? He thinks so as many sheeple cower.

Due to social hypnotism people are deadheads. Stop the debate--they just get irate--and go inside instead.

To be the man/woman of the hour, before idiots don't cower. Stand up to evil then blessings will shower.

The bondage of darkness is so strong they lose the will to obey--to do things God's way. It's denial/not ok.

The deep are seen as creeps. With the shallow they feel like strangers in a strange land--black sheep.

If we conform to groupthink we stay rinky-dink. Return to self for excellence and staying in the pink.

They make contact then inject their mental map. Why you need spiritual armor: you can't be zapped.

It's not good for men to talk like sailors. So why do you wanna copy them, you feminist derailers?

Everyone wants to be famous and it's embarrassing. They don't do a thing but take pics with out meriting.

SHAMELESS DEBAUCHERY

They're shameless in their debauchery--even proud. How foolish as they justify these things so loud!

Due to behavior of the people the land's become desolate. The princes rebel and they are inveterate.

Some women think they're supposed to be angry--all the time. Is this feminism, friends of mine?

HOW THEY RUINED US

Says the left: if you don't like that behavior you hate that person. "Newspeak" leaves me bereft.

Darkness blinds the eyes. That's why sinners are always zombies whether mean girls or violent guys.

Stop foolish flattery of supposed superiors. Gushing and fawning aren't the attributes of true leaders!

Children should be seen and not "herd". When groupthink runs rampant it's chaos and order's not preferred.

Inner emptiness from lack of people? See it's just social hypnotism then stand high as a steeple.

When good men do nothing, evil takes over. It's automatic, so either be firm with guests or get closure.

It's all about looks: selfies. Simultaneously our culture is getting even more shallow and selfish.

They flaunt themselves with smiles and style--legends in their own mind but still filled with guile.

These are the days that try men's souls. Non-reaction and equanimity in the face of hate are our goals.

Everyone wants to be famous, trendy, in the limelight, a friendly. They do nothing for it but pose--just blank entry.

Whatever they say they are, they're the opposite. Then they project it all onto you as a composite.

TYRANNY OF THE GROUP

The group keeps you down--un-renowned--as censorship and control blocks the winner's crown.

They have nothing but their group. That's why they hold on tight but to them you must not stoop!

HOW THEY RUINED US

Never suckup to those shunning you as corrupt. If shame keeps you hooked, repent then look up.

People are influenced away from self and God. Left to themselves it's natural though it does seem odd.

Does wife fight by calling the sheriff? A low blow, pure trouble with no merit: a kind of leverage or tariff.

I notice society's trends and the biggest one is people are busy socially but have few real friends.

Society is so messed up people don't see anything wrong with the things they do. Does this refer to you?

All they do is primp and take pictures of themselves. I go for the humble and serious: the magic elves.

People reflect their generation, to their detriment. For it always splits from the True Self: an impediment.

We're made crazy trying not to offend. This is stupid, friends: it warps speech (stops the gems).

Wealth came from being free. But now it's all leaving as we go under tyranny called "goodies for free".

Moral relativism makes certain types insane. When told "everything's equal" the brain warps in pain.

Denial is everywhere, it's called human psychology. We all make a box and stay there--that's our history.

SMARTER MEANS LESS POPULAR

The smarter you are the less popular. It wasn't this way before but now they only attend to the gossiper.

Feminism's made women whorish/mannish. The world needs decency and this other should be banished.

HOW THEY RUINED US

Leave behind the world of dust. They think they're special but that's just the outer crust (have no trust).

They're calling barbarity "good" just to be fair to all. That's the opposite to past eras when all stood tall.

One in five professors self-identify as Marxists, after 100+ million people were killed by this.

Many Mormons are liberal and don't realize it, thinking they're "good" for it.

They are told their true instincts are racist.

Since it's tied up in virtue signaling they can't see how liberalism's wrong: just "help" the throng.

Never envy the smiling trendies because most are in the cities and they'll be changed dangerously.

Let the trendy commies go to the cities they'll all be gone in these tragedies.

The good folk, the Christians--bitter clingers to our traditions--are in the small country towns fishin'.

Serious folk in true reality aren't smiling like Cheshire cats saying cheesecake and other fakes.

Every one in the pic is showing their teeth--a sign of aggression--and that's called socializing.

The world is full of young males causing all this trouble. It's all the same club whether ISIS or liberals.

PURITANISM: A RESPONSE TO CHAOS

Puritanism: a response to chaos. Cries for order emerge when surrounded by the lush and louse.

Democrats in Montana take more seriously defending Muslims than even our own constitution.

HOW THEY RUINED US

They're brainwashing us through cartoons. And most are dumb enough to accept this--buffoons.

We treacherously departed from the living God--our Father in Heaven replaced with the flawed.

There is nothing more unsettling and unwholesome than a whorish or mannish woman, amen?

Poetry is my solution for heartbreak when I've had all I can take. If happy, it would only be a fake.

Liars: It's all about getting buyers! Watch the leaders you hire and take note when decency expires.

Is it any wonder many are depressed? Stop bad leaders before they ruin and kill us at our foe's request.

If you're good at something just do that. Success is easy unless regulations make our dreams go splat.

Sometimes low self-esteem is a good thing, compelling constant improvement in dance or sing.

FAMOUS KNOW-NOTHINGS

Though famous he's an obvious know-nothing. But you're enamored cuz he's well known, how sickening.

If you were a true feminist you'd be acting feminine, not like a man--is this hard to understand?

Women have never been so abused nor poor. Result of feminism: close that door--not the way to soar.

Unless bully gets his way he's upset--that's liberalism—but smashing false concepts brings a serene ocean.

Must get rid of all Quisling traitors like Boehner--contributing to the destruction of a nation disfavored.

HOW THEY RUINED US

New Agers don't see how God's word and guns go together, how restraint makes birds of a feather.

If they call you a hater cuz you speak the truth, don't speak to them unless they apologize to you.

The youth seem all for these things, but not really. They've been hypnotized with slogans, silly.

The obvious is unseen until someone says it simply. My job: though it shocks it's really friendly, known quickly.

Always remember to be like children with hearts so tender: You must shut out the psychic offender.

Guns are the great equalizer for elderly and women. Need protection, thus gun grabbers are vermin.

New talk show with a trendy at the helm. Success without morals makes her so much less (low realm).

They love her cuz she says what they don't dare say. How does that make sense--are people swayed?

Regulations kill incentive then all goes dead: we're no more inventive. Solution: Pray to stay creative.

Have no bad associations with out honor. They support monsters and this makes them evil: about this, ponder.

THEY'RE ALL DUMBED DOWN

They're all dumbed down: they think they're smart with judgments unsound. Love God, be big in town.

Like a duck let it fall off your back. Some are angry--no tact. Everyone feels tension, that's a fact.

Though it seems we're entering hell, recall the tale of two cities: there's also jubilee, so come out of your shell.

HOW THEY RUINED US

Fill your cup with work then turn it off. Do it as a daily routine but you still need to relax, like golf.

If you disagree with one thing, it's war! This polarization I deplore. Keep to real friends, then soar.

Why are they angry? They're taught newspeak: they are their behavior, so criticize it = lost favor.

They think they control reality with thoughts. You can't--it's nuts--you only rise up by ridding ruts.

Contradictions resolved, a nugget comes out.

Don't seek fame, it's lame. Mind your rep with God (not man) or you'll go back from whence you came.

Much "acting out" is just copying the world. Forgive yourself for mimicry then your dreams unfurl.

To "love" them you must approve of everything they do. A lost opportunity--but I dig, why feud?

To tell the truth you may bring bad news. If it tell's em what's ahead (like abuse) they dare not refuse.

False accusations (making stuff up) justifies them doing bad things and the courts get rough.

COPYING MEN IS NOT FEMALE POWER

Women: how is copying men "female power"? Expanding your attributes is the woman of the hour.

Feminism: a failed liberal experiment. Women have never been so abused and poor, that's my sentiment.

Though nothing deep they're constantly on display--these creeps have nothing to say and stay low-pay.

It's the public's dumbness allowing this evil happening. For the same reason

HOW THEY RUINED US

they're snippy and snapping.

Don't go to their pages, don't stalk them in your rages. We're not in the dark ages, these behaviors have high wages.

All around people are panicking and that explains rough handling. Call on God, He'll be answering.

Even now with ultrasound they say it's not a baby. How can they sleep at night about this thing so shady?

How proud they are in their esprit d'corps (group). With them our liberty will droop and that's the true scoop.

Family Fascism is how they maintain the status quo and its dark, mean and discriminatory--an old story.

God, make men bold. For it's wimps and trendies who got us into this: to the enemy we've been sold.

Only anti-feminists are my "sisters". Not those encouraging bad trends like a wound that festers.

PSYCHOLOGY OF GANGS

Everywhere we see psychology of gangs. This signifies the implosion of society, at least birth pangs.

Obama was shutting down all the coal then giving it to friends with monopoly and jacked up prices as the goal.

Those wicked eyes and hearts: some family members are just plain evil but they control the people.

Just say it. Don't be bashful or fear offending, get a grip. Above all have courage and be bold, not "hip".

Feminism's made women mannish/whorish. They were more respected before--now they're anguished.

HOW THEY RUINED US

The feminist blogger looks down on women with husbands and kids. This phony is crazy, you dig?

Promises of conquest and grandeur: They'll do anything to be in the glare to be seen by the voyeurs.

He looks so perfect he's not seen as a madman--the superficial generation's into looks or Batman.

The mere fact that they love these stars indicates how dumbed down and demoralized they are.

There are times when the whole world's asleep. They can't boast what they've learned: blind sheep.

Give a bureaucrat power and he'll abuse it, excusing it. That's the police state: we must diffuse it.

In tyrannies no one tries a thing lest they become visible. Creativity is hampered by feeling vulnerable.

They make earth-shattering decisions through the left-brain: tyrants pulling our chain without refrain.

They moved the means into place, ready to squash the Ace. When that lid comes down, lost is the race.

The heckling is endless because it's mindless. In arrogant power we're becoming not more but less.

It's laughable but in this crazy climate even SHE can make it: Just eat right, look good or even fake it.

Be proud you're not as dumb as your gullible friends. You stayed centered, they followed trends.

HAUGHTINESS SHALL BE BROUGHT LOW

Their haughtiness shall be brought low. Human arrogance is always the problem we must outgrow.

HOW THEY RUINED US

They still like him for his reflected glory. That's humans all through history: misery, never victory.

The phonies stand in line for hours just to shake his hand. They love him though all they say is banned.

What turned me from liberalism? Hitting bottom on SIN. It takes what it takes to make you right again.

Martial Law: coding system to classify "hostile" and "friendlies"--not looking for crimes but permissive vs. enemies.

They scan the environment looking for anomalies (not bad guys). Then they focus and decide.

So much unnecessary hurt and pain: this is the outcome of feminism which you unwisely saw as gain.

The loving are the most terrible when it comes to tyranny so learn to see through labels of your enemies.

Appeasement brings only destruction but the liberal love song dominates as we go into election.

Put all horrors in the same bag and label it the latter days. This saves your nerves--it pays.

Latinos should realize their conservative values. Family, work, morality, God, freedom (virtues).

We're being bombarded--with chemicals, sick thoughts and evil trends all making us mentally retarded.

Plan: This is it: He's supposed to control our language, borders and culture but he does the opposite, ruining our future.

They have massive money, means and motive. This isn't going away--it's a barreling locomotive.

GOD KILS GIANTS WHO ARE AFTER US

HOW THEY RUINED US

The bigger the giant is trying to kill us, the more it conforms to Bible Stories where God shows up.

Have we reached the point of no return? Yet for God it's not impossible so for Him we all should yearn.

The dumbed down are in a trance. Thus, they could care less and will vote for anything, alas.

The police state is our scary fate because we weren't watchmen of our liberties or the forth estate.

We have both a constitutional and a divine right to feel secure with the freedom from fear.

He's anathema to everything America stand's for. He's being unmasked though, as evil to the core.

Every minute we're less legitimate: our demise is imminent as we endure hypocrites in increments.

You get to a point where you can't tell yourself stories anymore. Denial hurts--close that old door.

God's higher than current events. Scan the headlines but don't get hung up: look above (the God scent).

TYRANTS FEAR THE BIBLE

The ideas of the bible scare tyrants to death. It's the notion of God above man (the state) that they hateth.

A nation can survive fools and even the ambitious. But it cannot survive treason from within: the officious.

To keep the peace, keep a piece. Guns are equalizers for women and elderly: when guns go UP crimes decrease.

Political correctness opposes true liberalism which is liberty: It's plain tyranny--can't you see?

HOW THEY RUINED US

I'm so scared of these people. They have no morals, ethics, boundaries or empathy--they are evil.

Mexicans are into home and that means protection and freedom from regulation.

Free market and the constitution are the principals that made us rich. When they're gone we're in a ditch!

It's the deception, spinning and manipulating of liberals or it's solid coherence to principals.

Democracy is two wolves and a sheep voting for "what's for dinner". A republic is laws (that's the winner).

Liberty creates a cornucopia, tyranny creates a living hell--as they go into a shell bad acts are compelled.

History doesn't repeat, it rhymes. In all times people fake an image to hide their crimes.

Since tyranny is the default setting in governments, unless we guard those rights out goes our light.

With moral chaos, tyranny takes over. That's why elites condone sin and loafers: they want the changeover.

A great evil took over the land. Just as I had more than I could stand it got worse, murders or scams.

I was part of this evil too. I knew no boundaries, restraints nor rules and I learned it in the schools.

It was the implosion of society, a nation coming under judgment. It's a horrible thing--you would not like it.

Just because he's doing their dirty work doesn't make him less evil as he causes massive upheaval.

Fraud is the new cynical, taking everything that has value by Hill or Bill and what a bitter pill: hell.

HOW THEY RUINED US

In WWII we were warmly united but now we're divided so now's the time to be divinely guided.

In Dumb-land the smart are targeted. They seek solace so they get addicted, their work unmarketed.

WHEN WICKED RULE THE PEOPLE MOURN

When the wicked rule the people mourn and it's constant torture seeing their country scorned.

People are even losing their family for saying the wrong thing. That's how much this fascism stings.

Hill and Bill work magic--they can get away with anything. Not us--we get it for merely talking.

The world's slipping into total and complete depravity. That's the true human condition without morality.

Arrogant liberals, vituperative females: angry, self-righteous, pitiful.

Polled Americans don't care about our nose dive to the bottom. Dumbed down, they even call it "awesome".

We're becoming a predatory hell pit by any yardstick. It's happening so fast it could make us brainsick.

It's disgusting: this descent into lawlessness with no account or busting. In barbarism there is no trusting.

LIBERAL IDEOLOGY TRUMPS LOGIC

As with liberals ideology trumps logic, the results can be tragic. As denial becomes chronic it's like a tonic.

The lower the slime the greater the exposure. That's the way it works now as evil is loved and chauffeured.

With evil concepts they've all gotten cozier. In just a decade most all are

HOW THEY RUINED US

angrier and sinning is easier.

When evil rules there is no justice and people mourn: Eat our substance and ignore what's been sworn.

It has become a crime to think and say what you want. Suddenly you're marginalized as they taunt.

Zombies reject those who think differently. They're in a rigid groove so it behooves you to go gently.

Fake niceties mark the social world, also stupid cruelties which unfurl. Go solo, detach from the mindless swirl.

The "animating contest" is you becoming YOU by demanding your liberty. Win it now or die a wanna-be.

Genius sees everything in opposites. Whatever the herd thinks, they know the reverse is the positive.

We're waiting for next shoe to drop: Each one gets worse as society flops-- that's implosion we got.

In times of evil collective intuition is infectious. This is contagious enlightenment, in excess.

When big gov controls things you get real hurt. Without accountability they treat you like dirt.

The end of the family is the end of the transmission of sexual restraint which promotes big government I say.

A drowning man calls out for God while before then he was a fraud. We're deeply flawed, then awed.

Mixing the trivial with the important is another psychotic marker. And yet that describes TV news, a mocker.

A COUNTRY GOING INTO JUDGMENT

When a country comes under judgment the result is horrific debasement and

HOW THEY RUINED US

most are not ready, but absent.

That's the way it works: high on themselves but then they implode--when suddenly they've become old.

Just because he's cool doesn't mean he knows how to rule. The public are fools trained by schools.

Raise people's dignity and all this tyranny dissolves. It can't stand the light of day, so reveal it all.

The real man is strong and stable. Give up on all messers, procrastinators and losers if you're able.

Male power cleanses country of cowardice. Aren't we done being wimped, betrayed and powerless?

They've declared war on good people—Christians, gun owners, libertarians, pro-lifers and returning vets.

All should mourn the loss of freedom. For it's no small thing as we're stuck in bedlam and beaten.

Evil is unlimited without standards. That's why we're in a nose-dive to the bottom, going backwards.

Take freedom for granted--that's how you lose it, stupid. To stay free be watchmen, not insipid.

Liberals say you gotta break eggs to make an omelet--that's the ends justify the means argument.

Just as it gets too painful to watch God'll kick it up a notch and it's in our favor as they continue to botch.

FEMINIST ADVICE RUINS LIVES

She never wanted the divorce and he's devastated--so why did it happen? Feminist advice never gladdens.

The imperious laugh about things which are serious. This is so desensitizing

HOW THEY RUINED US

and cruel one gets delirious.

Free societies do not have "state ideologies" but government punishes thought without apologies.

Liberalism used to mean free thought and debate. Not anymore--you hold to the party line, a bore.

Having an opinion, just talking, knowledge or discernment is now "racist". This is scary and fascist.

They destroy traditional values so we don't feel normal--it's all overwritten to debunk role models.

The left is why we're sinking fast. I used to be a liberal, I know the spiel but that idiocy is passed.

They claim leftist ideas as their own. No, it's a hypnotic mantra inculcated over decades, full-blown.

Ideologies fog danger situations. That's why rising expectations are easily dashed (no foundations).

Genius knows truth is opposite to what "they" think. That's another way of sayin': herd reality stinks.

Due to surface status they are snobs. It's hard to take when already at odds or when there are no jobs.

They don't despise yet allow sins too. They shut their eyes since the axe hasn't fallen but it's going to.

It's earth shattering news but, they can't hear it. They're in a state of pliant acceptance, they don't fear it.

LIBERALS ARE LAWLESS

Liberals aren't into laws: they are lawless. Ethics, morals and standards are gone but also no more solace.

Liberal equals contradiction. That's because their self-image (loving) opposes

HOW THEY RUINED US

who they are: a fiction.

Women cajoled to abort or divorce are called "good", "worthy" or "trendy" but end sadly or in poverty.

Of course they disbelieve it--it's followed by jokes. Media is mixed-up so people fall back to their yokes.

Rome: Control the masses by keeping them stupid and self-indulgent but none avoids punishment.

The evil is not in bread or circuses but the willingness to sell their rights as free men for food/games. Cicero

Full bellies/excitement of games distracts men from those needs which games can never meet.

Worlds collapse when evil takes over. From county to state we need a makeover, with full exposure.

"Heckler's veto": whoever yells the loudest wins by being annoying like a mosquito--not peace but ego.

There's a point where silence rules. You can't say a thing without offence so save yourself from fools.

Freedom is like snow cones in hell. Without it man gets scared, no one cares, he's stuck in a shell.

Feminism ruined marriage. Women are taught to degrade their husbands, not nurturing: reality switches of witches.

If "they" don't know about it, it's not happening. So instead of studying they're napping (it's baffling).

Movies reflect and create culture: a feedback. They guide us into destruction or provide resolution.

TYRANNY OF THOUGHT

Tyranny trickles down to all levels: top to bottom, nothing left out as they rout

HOW THEY RUINED US

out rebels via goon devils.

When the herd calls it "beautiful", is it so? What of the rules of aesthetics--should that all go?

Forced to see it all "positively" they can't think critically, see through man nor overcome difficulty.

Forced to think "positively" they're zombies when it hits the fan. See the whole picture--think you can?

When does "positive" become refusal to accept valuable new information for a vital turn of direction?

Any attempt to impose standards gets you labeled a churchist finger-wagging old prune moralist.

In modernity, social standards makes you a moralist witch-hunter.

Just the fact they see you as bad is an insult so don't reply/it'll stop.

Hippies sitting around a table unwinding reality with relentless relativism, subjectivism and superstition.

Soon we couldn't judge a thing: type of floor, color of the door, assault on reality--loving what we abhor.

One toe in reality and the rest madness/subjectivism and now monogamy was repression, restraint prison.

The hippy's turning inside-out of the mental or artistic worlds brought madness/mental illness later.

They've created a culture war to control us. They've lied so much about our president/created a fuss.

Trump's no sexist, having appointed more high-powered women around him than any previous administration.

TOLERANT GENERATIONS THE MOST INTOLERANT

HOW THEY RUINED US

Tolerant Generations are the most intolerant of all: divorce, bullies and violence--everywhere a brawl.

When is "positive" a refusal to face reality? Life really sux at times for it's not all ONE thing but duality.

Being different gets you dis-owned. This social fascism is why we get cloned (why many get stoned).

It's a sorry state of affairs when we can't see evil cuz we're putting on airs. Better to be called squares.

Desperate to avoid disapproval they collapse everything in mind like the difference between good and evil.

What will save us? Men as real men and women as real women behind them-- the way of power, amen.

Only crap makes the news so avoid the blues/psychic bruise by stopping TV: more carefully choose.

You can't say anything, no kidding. More each day evil powers are forbidding. Solution: chilling.

While censuring they go along with new things and it gets crazier as they become less a king or queen.

When they take offense you feel dense but it's not you it's nonsense on attack as you get tense.

Look forward to your new life in heaven--where they won't be. That's valuable information for free.

BEING POSITIVE IS SELECTIVE DIS-ATTENTION

If being positive brings on selective dis-attention, warning: you'll lose the election or a new affection.

We're getting so afraid to speak the bloody truth lest when we call it uncouth they'll punch out a tooth.

HOW THEY RUINED US

They actually feel right being the thought police. It's getting so we can't say anything--please, let it cease.

Because they draw lines of clear restraint like a house gated, Christians are hated but it's not ill-fated.

.
They're proud of the very things of which they should be ashamed. They wear it like a badge of great fame.

Political correctness means you don't communicate about a thing: With this kind of censorship it's hard to be king.

Movie idols provide archetypes for the herd to follow. They are brilliant and wise or dark and shallow.

When you intrude they call you "rude" but they can interrupt, undercut and collude: the lawless brood.

Are your guests agents of calamity and woe? Do they cause trouble, is your time/money theirs to blow?

Once you get involved with that level it all spirals down to hell. Then it spreads in concentric circles like a spell.

The rare times they're nice we think "there is hope". But then we see it's all a ruse hiding the end of the rope.

Big Pharma sponsors most of TV. That's why every commercial is about drugs, see? Reject, be free.

PHARMACUCIA IN AMERICA

Mass shootings are always from mood-altering drugs like Xanax—every very single incident: facts!

They still love him after he does all this? They don't care about his dis as they fall into the abyss?

The more he sabotages the more they love him. Humans are a paradox: sycophants in an oven.

HOW THEY RUINED US

If you don't agree, you're out. They also want you friendless/jobless: a social gout (without clout).

Pharmacia numbs your children and robs them of their identity. It happened to me (I lost my destiny).

They cover it all up: they don't like you using the name. Why is this? Because they are so ashamed.

Reports leave us with less or no hope. The problems seem way beyond our scope: a deadly national soap.

Devils may win again--we may be that pathetic. What they've allowed is tragic and we should reject it.

Family: two dads, one mom and one dating another person. No wonder suicide's up: this is the reason.

From the most wonderful to the most horrible, overnight. It's like someone turned off a bright light.

They get power through class warfare, division, racial strife--these are not true liberals but a pack of criminals.

INSANITY IS A LOWER ARCHETYPE

Insanity is a sudden archetype exploding onto the scene. It's a lower strata in the brain revealing the fiend.

Insanity is a mal-adaptation to a sick system marked by flip-flops and sting-shots: happy then vehement.

These people are lax--they don't care about a thing! I have to forget them so my tender heart sings.

Evil is defended by the stupid, the naive and deniers. They'll believe any brutality is good--fools and liars.

Why can't people see evil? Because they're dense to the core, terrorized against seeing truth and more.

HOW THEY RUINED US

They think if it's not on the news, it doesn't exist. You gotta dig deep to get the truth or it's missed.

We've lost our greatness, we're under bondage: Total slavery and cruel reversals like an old adage.

Men who are good guys (over-solicitous partners): This wins the game but loses as they gotta try harder.

Authoritarian Cleptocracy: Put them under tyranny while stealing them blind and being very unkind.

They get so big and full of themselves: unproductive, petty, empty--the opposite to the magic elves.

If actions stem from ego they'll be futile. Why make embarrassing mistakes by doing things for approval?

That we're going down is no dispute. It hurts seeing the greatest getting the boot but get ready to uproot.

Liberals have always been anti-military so now we're weak sycophants having lost our peace and dignity.

Humans are only happy when inventing, freely expressing and daring--all crushed by the overbearing.

America had great industry--all their excellent thing, like their ministry--and thus they had victory.

TO LIBERALS ENDS JUSTIFY MEANS

To liberals "ends justify means" but no one sees the blood carnage in between--it's cold, and it's mean.

They were never in the military yet wanna have all these wars--not for our freedom but to settle old scores.

The worse things get the more power they get. It used to be you were fired but now all's in reverse: no debt.

HOW THEY RUINED US

It used to be if it happened on your watch you resigned or went to jail. Now you get a bonus, high-scale.

They actually think they're good. That's their identity despite narcissism and a heart dead as wood.

The mind wants justice and without it feels horrified. Then it just blanks it ALL out while truth is denied.

Dumb on history you're doomed to repeat it and I won't be part of that. Unplug from evil: drop the brats.

We can no longer say what we want. We have to tailor everything to what they think, like a sad haunt.

It's been about sixty years: collectivism, communitarianism then communism. Drip-drip now comes Statism.

A time will come when killing you will be a good thing. They know not what they do--murder or a fling.

He's impervious but all tyrants are that way. They gotta show they could care less--how they make hay.

Whether mad or happy depends on what news you watch--if bought they never report the botch.

Why show us her messy house--why wasn't she ashamed? Her mother would've but she's morally lamed.

Solve the paradigmatic confusion. Looking in all the wrong places the result is chaos and obtusion.

SCANDALS ASIDE THEY STILL LOVE POWERS THAT BE

Scandals yet they still love the powers that be. The worse things get the more they're seen as daddy.

They have drones the size of a fly--go behind doors, kill you or spy. To our freedoms say bye-bye.

HOW THEY RUINED US

There's a charisma to the fakery but image-magic's not bravery. Seen through clear eyes it's buffoonery.

They come with many men. This is the day your life changes suddenly so enjoy each day until then.

Feminism is anti-family: As women take the upper hand and bash men, the nice ladies are anomalies.

How bad it is when a culture replaces one group for another. It's all for power pitting brother against brother.

If authorities have a low I.Q. don't debase yourself to better look up to them, but choose breakthrough.

As his ratings plummet there's a mass readjustment to a new beat: revitalization movement vs. the elite.

When things get bad the herd is like a flock of birds flying in perfect unison and changing as a unit.

They either get better or worse. Lukewarm doesn't exist--just milquetoast people where love is a farce.

They aren't even "there" so find people to validate their illusion--deadheads causing more confusion.

The washed-out wimps--look at those in congress. They lay down to be weak, they allow the mess.

BE SCARED OF DENSE

If you're not scared you don't know what's going on. TV news is falsehood--not where you belong.

Okay so you don't wanna hear it. Though it's horrible news (the truth) just listen then pray to God's rescuing spirit.

Will tyranny be better with a female in a pink pant suit? No it will worsen as a she-brute makes us go mute.

HOW THEY RUINED US

Liberal women turning from Hillary didn't want their sons and husbands to endure femi-nazi tyranny.

You're a mean-spirited, small time, leftwing fanatic incapable of leading a nation. Not misogyny, it's *you*.

When you lose you don't whine or you seem like a bigger loser--we woulda had that for 4-8 years!

Biggest lie in Hillary's book: where she lays blame on anyone else for losing when she's just a crook.

Calling Trump a "white supremacist" and outrageous statements like that.

Hopefully you're gone forever but not before more fruitless endeavors.

Start a race war: It is possible to do this just by baiting, threatening, rewarding, trending and fear.

A big fat gut with finger in nose insults you then insists you forget it while he talks other folderol.

They became adversarial, not us. They picked a bone and had a grudge but we overcame by reading Drudge.
When the pages are forced to do bad things they rebel on constitutional grounds and win over kings.

They're gonna do it whether we like it or not. We've lost all power--our influence has turned to rot.

Your problem is trying to make them "see". They can't, all they see is "me" and that's wisdom for free.

THEY JUST KNOW THEY'RE RIGHT

You can be certain you're right and be 100% wrong. The true scientist knows this but not the throng.

The more complaints aired, the greater protection for human rights in that country. So speak, urgently.

HOW THEY RUINED US

First we're a rare experiment then it's (authoritarian cleptocracy, crony capitalism): gangster government.

It's not about resistance but of survival. You must stand up for right or slip down more into evil.

The mental problems from adapting to an angry feminist female--that is the weakening, the final nail.

Tyranny's strategy: get everyone on the dole then pull the plug as all collapses--a sinking ship of asses.

Enlighten the people and tyranny disappears. Teach them about dignity and destiny and hear their cheers!

Americans prefer crap to real news--a bad sign as the country's bruised while they snooze after booze.

We've had a setback--it's hard to stomach. Wake up America, with God we can have a comeback!

Liberalism is an induced character disturbance. They lie, cut corners (cheat) and call it "abundance".

The post-war generations got slack, lax and inexact. They got sloppy, fat and mopey--that's a fact.

Making you think like them is their one crusade--because the wrong haven't the tools to dissuade.

FROM THE SIXTIES: SLOPPY, DIRTY, UNPRETTY

From the sixties women became sloppy, dirty and un-pretty. This was the feminist influence--a pity.

They're gonna do what they want whether we like it or not. Those in power control thought and we cry a lot.

She seeks to make me think like her. That's her goal backed with gossip from other dream-smashers.

HOW THEY RUINED US

To be politically correct, we lost our country--the only one this stupid as the world sees us as nutty.

Appointed a four-star admiral (she can't fly a plane nor pilot a ship) but complained of sex harassment.

Just as he fails Obamanoids dig in more. That's how demagoguery works, like a pimp to the whore.

It's how they've been taught. From sinister forces these were the lies they bought--it takes a high mind to not.

Bottom of the rabbit hole is satanism/pedophilia and everyday you see em flushed out in America.

Warning: The satanists look normal, smiling, trendy and good but the end is terrible and alarming.

Sexualization of children combined with tolerance training is the power's pedophile-normalizing.

Teaching sex acts to 5 year olds are pre-acts of pedophilia: grooming and sexualization in America.

Teaching sex acts to five year olds is pedophile training and grooming: that's what your gov is doing.

SATANISTS WANT TO CONTROL EVERYONE

Satanists wanna control everyone but we just wanna be left alone.

You're not a megalomaniac narcissist sociopath so you're blind to how they get into power/become legends.

So arrogant she won't go away, clinging to relevancy. They love her cuz she represents history? Must be.

Like Hitler, deep state losers are so arrogant they can't believe the world is turning against them.

HOW THEY RUINED US

Unable to believe they lost they can't move on, living in a nonexistent world plus we're onto them.

Sociopaths believe a lie--they cannot ever admit they're wrong (that's what makes them one).

You can't tell them anything, the leftist cult. The more delusional they get the more you're at fault.

Poets get on "lists". It's due to their powerful less-is-more impact from novel twists. Even after death they persist.

You must block the trash: low minds--the brash with whom you clash. It's spiritual being bashed!

Suddenly the army appears on your street. That's how it works, and it's the military--it won't be sweet.

The left minimizes all dangers: relaxed all vigilance against gangs, terrorists, felons, strangers.

Avoid futile debate with ideologues (nuts) for their thinking is third rate. Be nice but show them the gate.

Never minimize effects of futile debate. They won't change so don't take the bait, keep to high fate.

Leaving California because of all you liberals. No wonder you're banned in other states especially by locals.

Any gov healthcare (without competition and profit-motive) will be sub-standard (the worst is cancer).

Leftists should think about Hitler--do they wanna repeat all that? It's national socialism, ding bats.

Conservatives and liberals are polarizing more than ever but the former can debate and be very clever.

How a country goes bankrupt: gradually at first, then suddenly. But success too: subtly then utterly.

HOW THEY RUINED US

Their lies are preposterous! Only a fool would believe this especially after all those capers so monstrous.

POLITICANS GROVEL TO HOLLYWOOD SCUM

Politicians grovel to movie stars who grovel right back: a mean ploy to make us feel separate, sad sacks.

Before its fall Rome had entertainment for the masses. Thus absorbed they missed the curses.

Hey fake trendies: Your reflected glory blinds you to your abnormalities--you are dangerous enemies.

After all that stress we have to convalesce. Repeat trauma: it's been years of the same lousy mess.

Yes impeach, I beseech: It's our constitutional right and duty to cut evil ties then ban the leech.

The more Hillary whines the more it's like OJ hunting for the real killers. Mark Steyn

First day Hillary's book goes 50 % off cuz no one's interested.
To the left, sex with children is just another boundary to be swept away. Academia: the child is prey.

Mature men like power/maturity but pedophiles like children cuz it's satanic: want their energy.

THEY SAY "PEACE" THEN DESTRUCTION COMES SWIFTLY

They clamor for peace and safety then destruction comes upon them swiftly.

Heard tonight: Abort your white baby, whites are bad, the world will be better off without whites.

Break up the nuclear family and the boys become criminals, the girls sexual slaves: it's predictable.

HOW THEY RUINED US

Women feeling vulnerable become susceptible to grooming or pedophilia gangs: that's just logical.

Frisco cops say: don't lock car door cuz they'll break in anyway.

All of our youth are being targeted and turned into thugs because it's the fad and it's bad.

The black looting is all ok cuz it's been media-spun that way: just getting even with the rich guy.

Wow: It's only the white people who are being beaten and hung now not the other way around.

Youtube wants a white child being hung to be the main trending video. Why?

Low income groups are more susceptible to tribalism and brainwashing with democrats behind em.

Feinstein: If you're a Christian you can't be trusted in judiciary. Anti-Christian venom: What if Muslim?

It's being culturally pushed to go out and loot white areas--you know the left is behind it in America.

A culture protected from offense encourages looking for more offense cuz it's superior to be victims.

They killed all the traitors who let em into the castle because they were the treacherous unfaithful.

LEFTISTS ARE NOT "HUMANITARIANS"

Leftists think they're the humanitarians of all time and yet that ugliness comes out, so unrefined.

Obama had a field day taking a sledge hammer to all America represents--did you come to her defense?

As Obama was dismantling America the media leftists loved it. Now they have nothing/can't take it.

HOW THEY RUINED US

75% say bypassing congress is not how gov should work. Feeling powerless, they're going berserk.

Outrageous: It's obscene our president didn't help the proud marine imprisoned by foreign fiends.

We've only just known our enemies were paid. Now let that ol' American ingenuity come to our aid.

It's not about "the children" but our lost sovereignty as a nation and the democrats winning elections.

America meant these things: self-determination, equal rights and wealth creation without strings.

Americana is: adapt, overcome, improvise. Why we won the high prize: we saw through evil's lies.

Don't blame dems, the reps are bought too. It's all the same club--global, tyrannical and angels are few.

Great cruelty has taken over society. Callous, lewd too--so much impropriety is a reaction to anxiety.

Big government is from hyper sexualized childhood--that's education understood.

We believed in property and family rights, right to defense and local control. No more, we're poor.

We're falling off a cliff, not of our own making but those who call themselves our reps. Solution: get hep.

Unless it's about the criminal takeover and police state, turn off the news--it's all fake, dead weight.

The drills are an acclamation. They're getting us used to their presence and terror without cessation.

It's a crisis (but manufactured) as they act as saviors and things spiral down--

HOW THEY RUINED US

but with God, we've won.

TRENDIES LOVE DECADENCE

Trendies are hypnotized by entertainment decadent society. There's no waking them, blind from anxiety.

Categorizing by groups not the individual is racism--like you seeing me as white not who I am.

We never knew how lucky we were--freedom put us under a spell but now it's a scary time from hell.

They don't worry cuz their friends aren't worried. That's the contagion of madness--carefree, unhurried.

Admit we're into tyranny and we have a chance to beat it. They're ready to drop the hammer, believe it.

SIGNS OF TYRANNY CREEP

California's rolling blackouts are there so you'll accept having no power so you'll pay more for it: clever.

Black people are no longer the victims of systemic racism, they are the beneficiaries of it. Mr. Reagan

RACISM: Don't study, that's too white. Don't speak well, dress nice or come on time--that's too white.

White people aren't racist, their weak--so with false accusations of it they cave in/don't speak.

White people just wanna live their own life to EXCEL but then they're accused of racism and going to hell.

HOW THEY RUINED US

Free stuff for everyone, freedom for no one. Remember the good ol' days of independence, liberty, fun?

Democrat convention: "low-energy speeches, shoddy productions, empty rhetoric, bizarre performances".

Obama's pixie dust at the convention tonight was more like sand in your eyes. Laura Ingraham

Platitudes heaped on cliche's smothered in a thick sauce of self-righteousness/stupidity. Tucker on dems

The astounding thing is how shamelessly they lie. Their goal is complete reality inversion. Tucker Carlson

They don't tell small lies, when it comes to democrats they go all the way-- guess we should admire their audacity.

Through Freudian transference, they displace their own sins onto you--thereby cleansing their consciences too.

Bad leaders: The only time Michelle Obama was proud of her country was when her family got to run it.

They get meaner and meaner but Trump ALWAYS wins out over them--no worries, that's the pattern.

They've fallen for the idea you can't criticize black women who are running or in power, no matter how low.

The biggest reason we reject democrats is they say nothing about the violence in their own cities. Rudy Giuliani

America is burning for one reason only: the democrats have pro-criminal, anti-police policies.

HIGH-CAR/B/LOW-FAT AND FIT?

Get your junk food way down and there's no need for creams and moisturizers for your dry aged skin.

HOW THEY RUINED US

How to heal someone: Stop poisoning them then give em starch like they enjoyed when they were young.

Apple juice, fruit spread on bread and later your meal: rice, corn, beans, rice noodles or spuds.

Now that's the main food on this continent. That's how you view it, then you forage for the lesser fruit/herbs.

Or cereal with rice milk, bananas, raisins, collagen, lotsa white sugar--filling the glycogen, energizing.

Spanish rice with salsa, refried beans with onions: sounds good doesn't it but NOT guacamole--give that up.

When going lowfat. No avocado, oily fish, cheese or dairy, oils of any variety. Then reverse back into high fat see.

You want SWEET or complex carb going sugary. THIS is what we run on: glucose gives us energy.

If you love rice you can love SALTY too, that's ok. But not OILY--many restaurants oil the rice, it's shiny.

I put nut-butters and coconut creams in smoothies for calories & a high-fat diet has dairy like cheese see.

HIGH ON REVERSAL DIETING

A genius is simply someone who's up all night and works all day too. He IS the work/writes what comes thru.

What is the true definition of pumpernickel and WHY is it the only acid-binding bread, and are they truly it?

They say you can't escape SOY. I do, there's NO SOY in apple juice, raisins, bananas, rice, corn or beans.

When it comes to correct foods, put all else aside and just concentrate on starches of that continent.

HOW THEY RUINED US

I ignore outer aisles of produce, meat, dairy, bakery and just do the inner: rice/beans/corn/juices/sucrose.

When it comes to food we want satiety and security, which is predictability. I Stick to fat so I won't be hungry.

Pancakes for breakfast: why not--It's a matter of grains go sugary: glucose is what creates our energy.

GLYCATION: MEATS ARE AGING

AGING comes from glycation. ZERO glycation foods are white rice, white sugar then there are fruit/grains.

Near Zero Glycation: Oatmeal, white rice, popcorn, sugar, bread. Sugar has no glycation--imagine that!

All those high-fat fruit deserts were so self-sabotaging, I can still remember the abdominal full feeling.

RAW chocolate, coconut creams, various oils and butters made from nuts and seeds: all AGING [glycating].

Meats shoot the glycation index up to 9000+ from zero. Now we can see the aging effects of meat eating.

I had always been taught that it was sugar shooting up glycation [aging] but here sugar is ZERO, see?

Barney Fife was skinny as a rail and he had THREE lumps of sugar in his coffee/no cream in every cup.

The CURE-ALL is sugar, white rice, fruit, fruit juice and GRATITUDE every moment. Durianrider

Now it doesn't even matter if it's pumpernickel. All bread is near-zero glycation [this is life-saving material].

Scrap all diet/aging theories you know. It's all GLYCATION and each food has a number: so easy to follow.

HOW THEY RUINED US

Who cares about vitaminerals when it's GLYCATION that makes us old, wrinkled, dry and miserable?

You aren't "fit" if suicidally depressed. Your mental health should follow the physical, feeling blessed.

Eat more fat, you develop insulin resistance making you anabolic [dying]--it shows in absolutely everything.

People resemble a bucket of KFC with their arms/legs sticking out. It's not sugar it's this stuff. Durianrider

They blame the sugar, not the fat in the cookies and candies that make em palatable. Sugar alone is the fuel.

SUGAR is simply the current scapegoat. People love their fats and they justify that in "science" talks.

RICE, CORN AND BARLEY

The most amazing feats of athletic performance are always done by starch-eaters: rice, corn and barley.

ALL winning endurance athletes live on starch while the losers usually live on meat and dairy.

The greatest/phenomenal athletes were the "barley eaters". They were happy all the time and deep sleepers.

I drink apple juice all day and night. It's the King of the Fruits so I feel very complete and completely high.

Most people won't completely change their diet to avoid a few wrinkles but the saints choose beauty.

GLYCATION equals shit skin. To avoid these signs of aging I'd do anything like any true artist at the end.

Don't botox out laugh lines and necessary creases but all in all your skin will be ageless, it's my promise.

HOW THEY RUINED US

Aging is from GLYCATION, glycation, glycation which doesn't come from sugar but fats--check the chart son.

Yet SUGAR is the trendy enemy, not fats cuz they are delicious and people eat what they want sis.

STORE STARCHES. Barrels of organic corn kernels, organic jasmine or basmati white rice--it's DELICIOUS.

It's not the sun wrinkling everything up it's the GLYCATION then the sun just toughens and dries it stiff.

When sugar links with protein there is elastosis as the elastin clumps up in this major characteristic of aging.

Keep the fat out and eat the sugar as your fuel--tho' all online blames the sugar for these signs of aging.

SUGAR IS THE FUEL

You could eat the fat/protein without sugar, but the glycation index from meat shoots sky high anyway dear.

High carb is low glycation, low carb is high glycation and it's that by definition. For skin the China Study has won.

Glucose is glucose so even if it's processed carbs it's still has glycation at near-ZERO while it energizes you.

You CAN reverse glycation by going lowfat. The linkages and elastosis stops and it goes out.

TERSE VERSE BEFORE INTERFERENCE

I don't want all your words I want TERSE VERSE cuz I ain't got time and meaning comes first.

I write like way this to subvert argument before they have a chance to: terse, quick and laconic.

HOW THEY RUINED US

While great books have been banned like Huck Finn they allow pornography in the schools/sin.

Just about all are hypnotized by the "All Is One" false cosmology: the 100 year plan to make us crazy.

You like open borders? You like letting criminals and killers back out? You must be a democrat.

Liberals have filthy minds from what they accept then put it on your back: what they do in private.

You have two against one--a Cinderella Syndrome--and it's the most obdurate of all sick systems.

They had all the power. They controlled reality--who I was--and that was my life until they expired.

THE HERD IN WORDS
HIX POLITIX
HOW THEY RUINED US
JUST SKIP DINNER
LE FEMME AND THE COMMUNIST SPIRIT
LIBERAL CHAOS & ROT
LIBERAL DOUBLETHINK
LIBERAL GALL 1 & 2
LIBERAL SHOVE-DOWNS
LOCK YOUR GATE
LOSERS and Femme Fatales
MANUAL FOR SUPERIOR MEN
MODERN ART FROM HELL
MOSTLY FAKE
NOTES TO CHAMPS 1 & 2
OVERCOME FRENEMIES
PC MAKES US CRAZY
PEOPLE ARE CRUEL
PEOPLE PROBLEMS 1 & 2
PERSECUTED GENIUIS
POLI-PSYCH MYSTERIES
PRETENTIOUS SLOBS
QUEEN BEE
RED NEW DEAL
RETURNING TO FIRST NATURE
SEASON OF TREASON
SEPARATE MEANS HOLY
SOCIAL HYPNOTISM
SOLITUDE SOLUTION
SUPERCILIOUS
THE SCHOOLS SCREWED EM UP
TOAD TO PRINCE
TRIALS CYCLES
TRUMP VS. GROUP
TRUST IN TRASH
THE TRUTH ABOUT PEOPLE
UNDERHEANDEDLY CLEVER
WALK TALL WITHIN WALLS
WE'RE NOT ALL ONE
WINNERS SKIP DINNER
WORK OR SMERK

KAREN KELLOCK PH.D.

M.S. Political Science, San Diego State. Ph.D. in Psychology, University of California Irvine. Postdoctoral: UCI School of Medicine, Dept. of Psychiatry [NIMH Grants]. Developed the Debris Theory of Disease, a theory of system pathology in 120 books and 22 textbooks for the general public. The theory has a general formula: All disease is obstruction, all recovery is elimination, all success is attraction. The three obstructions are people, habit and food. Remove obstruction and snap to your goals, waiting in the wings.